You are My SignShine!

You are My SignShine!

A complete guide to using Sign Language to connect and communicate with hearing babies & children.

Best steps, studies, tools, games, activities, and pictorial dictionaries.

Etel Leit, M.S.

This book contains advice and information related to language development of babies and children. It is not intended to subtitle for medical or developmental advice. Consult your pediatrician and/or child's therapist should you have any concerns or before adapting any developmental program to verify that your plan is suitable for your child.

Published by SignShine®

Text and Photographs Copyright ©2015 by Etel Leit

You are My SignShine!
A complete guide to using Sign Language to connect and communcate with hearing babies & children.

ISBN-10: 0988595206
ISBN-13: 978-0-9885952-0-0

All rights reserved. Printed in the United States of America. No part of this publication may be reproduced, stored in a retrieval system or transmitted in any form or by any means, electronics, mechanical, photocopying, recording or otherwise, without the written permission of the publisher.SignShine and associated logos are the trademarks of SignShine®.

For more information regarding permission contact SignShine®. www.SignShine.com

Cover design by James Kirtley

Typesetting by Robert J. Peterson.
www.robertjpeterson.com

Printed in the U.S.A.

For Zoë & Dylan,
who teach me unconditional love
beyond words

Table of Contents

Preface
The Importance of Signing: Etel's Story   17

Section One
Signing Guide   23

Chapter One:
Before We Start   25

1. Fact or Fiction?   25

Busting the 5 Myths of Baby Sign Language   25

2. Parenting Starts with Language: 29

Why Sign with Your Hearing Child?   29

3. The History of Baby Signing   32

The Women's Perspective…   33

4. When to Start Signing?   35

5. Benefits to Signing with Babies and Toddlers   36

Chapter Two:
Let's Start: Tips and Tools 39

1. Twelve Simple Steps to Signing   39

2. First Five Tips for Beginning Signers   44

3. Five Stages of Baby Signing   45

4. Face-to-Face Time   48

Chapter Three:
Beyond MILK and BABY 51

1. Family Business: Signs of Love   51

2. Signing in Bilingual Settings   54

3. Teaching Manners   57

Chapter Four:
Let's Play 61

1. Signing Games and Activities   61

2. Ten Ideas and Activities to Promote Verbal Communication   69

3. Teaching the Concept "More": MORE is Not the First Sign 72

4. More Bubbles and Creative MORE 73

Tips for Bubbly Success 75

Chapter Five:
From Signs to Words: Literacy Skills and Signing 77

1. Use Signing to Emphasize Learning: 79

2. Reasons to Sign with Books 79

3. How to Sign with Books 80

4. Opportunities to Sign with Books 81

5. Signing with Verbal Children 83

Chapter Six:
Who Else Signs? 87

1. Caregivers Sign 87

2. Educators Sign 89

3. Signing with Special Needs Children 90

How Can Signing Help? 91

But Wait, I Have Some Questions! 93

Who Can Use Sign Language? 96

Chapter Seven:
Ask 101

1. Why Choose Baby Signing? 101

2. Questions Everyone Asks 103

3. Five Reasons to a Take Group Sign Language Class 106

Section Two
SignShine®'s Families
Real Signing Stories 109

Signing Saved Nathaniel from Cancer 111

Bilingual Mother-In-Law 113

Grandparents Appreciate Manners 115

A Sign of Hope 117

Alex Signs Concept of More 121

… Alex Continues to Sign   123

Daddy and Me   125

Aiden Uses his Signs   127

My Special Benefits of Signing   133

Introducing Signs   135

Daddy's Reaction to Signing… The Miracle   137

Signing Eases Terrible Twos for a Single Mom   139

Sebastian's Head Start   141

Eugene's Miracle   143

Our SignShine Story   145

Understanding Language Before Verbal Words   147

Section Three
Pictorial Dictionary 151

Cheat Sheet: Illustrated Dictionary   153

Family Signs   155

Concept Signs   163

Playtime Signs   165

Bedtime Signs   171

Color Signs   175

Feeling & Emotion Signs   179

Section Four
Your Signing Story 185

Preface
The Importance of Signing: Etel's Story

We all want to be understood. Think about the last seriously frustrating conversation you had with someone close to you – your mother, your sister, your spouse, your best friend. Chances are the thing that bothered you most was the sense that the person you were arguing with just didn't understand you.

Now imagine that you didn't even have words to try to get your point across - or worse, that you didn't possess even the power to voice distinct sounds. Imagine how frustrating *that* would be. What would you do to try to get your message heard? Yell? Cry? Throw a fit?

That's what it's like to be a baby or a toddler, who just wants someone to listen to him but doesn't yet possess the sophisticated language to express his needs, desires, and feelings. And when children are frustrated,

Signing "book" with Zoë.

the adults around them are too, spending hours trying to figure out how to soothe that sobbing infant or calm that out-of-control toddler.

But what if you could stop the sobbing before it started or cut off the tantrums before they began? What if you could figure out a way to truly communicate with your child, creating a positive environment in which you could resolve your power struggles in an easy and respectful way, satisfying and honoring both of your needs and feelings?

When I was pregnant with my daughter, I spent hours researching language acquisition in children because I knew that my daughter would be raised in a primarily English-speaking environment despite the fact that my own first language is Hebrew. My research led me to signing as a way to help bridge my daughter's dual-language heritage. The more I learned about signing with babies and children, the more I realized I wasn't just having a personal epiphany but a professional one as well. I wanted to combine a lifetime devotion to languages with my newest passion – motherhood! And so with the birth of my daughter, my business SignShine® was also born.

As I started to sign with my daughter, I was awed by the deep communication benefits and extraordinary intimacy between us that signing together brought. Teaching other parents to sign only reinforced my beliefs about the power of signing with children.

Signing "cow" with Dylan.

Not only was I witnessing the same miracles of communication that I'd experienced with my own children, played out again among my students, but I was constantly being asked for signing tricks and tools to combat common parenting concerns. Offering signing solutions came easily to me, but I was surprised to find that practicing signing in this way was not part of the larger "Baby Signing" industry that was growing around me while I built my own business – and still isn't, today.

As a person who teaches both parenting classes and signing with children classes, I have seen firsthand how much easier it is for parents and other caregivers to interact and engage with children in a positive and relaxed manner when they and their children have learned to sign. Signing is miraculous in that it offers children both a simple *vocabulary* and the power of a more sophisticated *conceptual* manner of communication. A ten-month old who signs "MILK" can easily ask for his bottle without having to resort to tears; a toddler who can sign "HELP" can express her frustrations with not being able to stack one red block atop another without screaming for assistance at the top of her lungs.

The effects of empowering parents and children to truly communicate through sign cannot be overstated. When a child signs, not only does she feel "heard," but she feels *safe* and *secure*, and the trust she feels radiates out towards anyone with the tools to "talk" with her. Anyone who shares her new language can benefit from this bond. I have seen fathers who previously felt "left out" from the special closeness between their children and their wives use the miracle of signing to develop and deepen their relationship with their child. I have seen the same miraculous relationships develop between children and grandparents, other caregivers, and teachers. And I have been told again and again how communication through sign has helped adoptive parents feel they bonded with children whom they worried might not attach to them as deeply as they'd witnessed in other families.

My experience in the field has convinced me that there exists a deep desire among parents and caregivers to learn whatever skills necessary to will enable them to better connect – and communicate – with the children they love. This book presents signing as a meaningful parenting tool that is fun, easy, and fast to learn – exactly what busy adults (and their children!) need.

That's why I wrote this book (which I call Etel's Book). I wanted to offer parents an alternative to the simple vocabulary lists and faux-sign language systems that provide little more than gimmicky support to busy parents seeking deeper guidance for connecting with their kids. That's why this book isn't simply an illustrated guide to "Baby Signing" but rather a parenting book about communicating with children of all ages, using true American Sign.

Inside these pages, you'll find information compiled from years of experience: tips, techniques, studies, games, activities, stories, how-to quick sheets, and so much more. If you are taking SignShine's class, this book will guide you along with our amazing curriculum.

It is an honor to be with you as you begin your Baby Sign Language journey.

Let the Sign Shine,

Section One
Signing Guide

Chapter One:
Before We Start

1. Fact or Fiction?
Busting the 5 Myths of Baby Sign Language

"I've heard that signing delays speech. Are you concerned?" "He's only a child. Why push him?" "We tried that, but it just doesn't work." "We already speak two languages in our home, so I don't want to confuse my daughter."

TRUTH BE TOLD, I LIKE it when people question what we're doing. It challenges me to stay current on the research, and it reminds me of all the reasons I believe in what we do. Demystifying the idea of using sign language with babies and children is yet another way to encourage parents on their path to creating strong bonds with their kids. The benefits of signing are endless, and I've seen family after family **thrive in their ability to communicate with their children at an early age.**

So let's take look at the most common myths of signing with babies and children:

Myth #1:
Using Sign Language Delays Speech

Not only do signing babies speak earlier, but research indicates they have higher IQ scores – by an average of twelve points at age eight. Why? When you sign with a child, you also say the word out loud. **Parents who sign tend to verbalize words more often than parents who do not sign**: "Do you want MILK? MILK? Here is your MILK." Children who hear words repeatedly will themselves repeat them.

Myth #2:
He's Already Talking Now; It's Too Late.

Even when children are in the early stages of verbalizing, they cannot say complete, clear sentences. The act of learning to speak fluently is a long process. But babies and children do have clear thoughts and sentences that they want to articulate. Gross motor skills develop before the fine motor skills involved in phonetic actions (moving tongues and mouths in the proper way to create speech). **Babies can communicate with their hands before they are verbally capable of articulating their thoughts.** Does BaBa mean Ball? Bath? Bunny? If your son or daughter is starting to form vowels and consonants into words, signing will help him or her to be precise.

Myth #3:
We Are Pushing Our Kids Too Much.

Signing is one of the most instinctive things that kids do – naturally. Think about what babies do to communicate their needs before they can talk. When they want you to look at something, they point. When they want to be picked up, they longingly put their arms in the air. **Sign Language simply fleshes out natural tendencies and gives them more options to communicate in a way that is developmentally possible.** It's not as if kids are learning a complex, ancient Roman language using flashcards and rote memory! Signing is simple and natural.

Myth #4:
Sign Language Is Hard!

Signing with hearing babies and children is different than signing with someone who is deaf. Although both situations use American Sign Language based signs, when we sign with hearing children, we are only using the key word or words in the sentence (a fantastic way to develop literacy skills). **Signing is one of the easiest languages to learn.** Take it from me; I've had the chance to learn four different languages with four different alphabets. Fortunately, several of the words used in signing are iconic and make sense. The sign for MILK, for example, looks like you're milking a cow. Even very young children can remember several different signs.

Myth #5:
It's Not a Good Use of Time (Something I Have So Little of!)

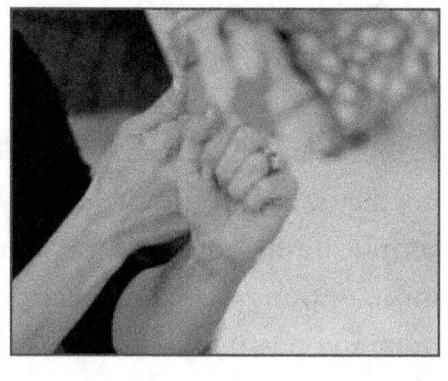

Signing has emotional and social benefits that can make your overall experience as a parent much more positive. Signing with your child can be a *fun* part of your daily life, just like everything else you do with your child. It provides the best of all worlds–**a meaningful way to communicate**, a game-like activity to do together, an informal teaching tool, and a means to building a close bond from early on. I still hear comments and questions like these, although fewer now that that signing has become more mainstream. Just a few years ago, people were puzzled about signing with babies and children. Some even thought that my daughter was deaf when I signed with her in public. Thankfully, **today, Sign Language has proven itself as amazing tool to communicate with hearing babies and children.** And because of the proof, the resources, the press, and the support, all continue to grow with each passing day.

Understanding your child and being understood as a parent are at the core of any meaningful relationship, so I applaud your efforts as you learn and teach this beautiful language!

2. Parenting Starts with Language: Why Sign with Your Hearing Child?

> *"I cannot wait for Emily to start having a real conversation with me, so I can finally understand what she wants. I know she understands the basics words when I talk, but all she does is point! I've read that she will start talking when she is about 18 months, but that even then, it won't be clear. Do I really have to wait that long to understand what she says?!"*

Most parents are impatient to "speak" with their pre-verbal children to connect with their kids on a conversational level. Many are convinced that they'll have to wait and wait and wait until their children are capable of producing vocal language. Then, imagine their surprise when I suggest using ASL as a way to communicate with their hearing children – not just as a short-term gimmick but as a way to capitalize on children's natural abilities and tendencies to physically make their own communication practice from the earliest age. For instance, most children lift their arms in the air towards an adult when they want to be picked up – that's a child's first sign!

Other parents worry that their children have more to say to them than they have the power to understand—they long for the day when their child will ask for *MILK* by name. Rather than crying and gesturing randomly until Mom or Dad figure out, through a painful process of elimination, what their child wants, these parents may discover signing as a way to offer their children a simple language tool to ease needs-based negotiations. Too often though, they abandon signing as soon as their children begin vocalizing language. In fact, most of the literature available to parents who sign with their children advocates giving up signing when children begin to speak.

This preference for "Baby Signing" over "signing with children" seems to grow out of a fear that signing with children will somehow stunt a hearing child's verbal development or that signing stops having any beneficial effects for children or parents once they start to speak. I find this belief strange, considering that research regarding signing with children shows that continuing to sign with speaking children actually acts as an effective tool for expanding kindergarteners' receptive and expressive English vocabularies and raises their emergent reading level, too. (Daniels, Marilyn, *Dancing with Words: Signs for Hearing Children's Literacy*.)

In fact, my experience has shown that offering a hearing child ASL as a language tool can be leveraged even further by using ASL as a meaningful communication tool well past infancy. Using ASL with your family establishes the importance of meaningful communication among family members as a lifelong practice from the earliest days. Signing allows adults to teach children complicated concepts well before the verbal equivalents can be understood and encourages a breadth of conversation that is unavailable to parents who rely solely on the verbal language their children possess. Because signing with children offers them a world of language they may still be unable to verbalize, signing deepens the communicative connection between children and adults and helps prevent "remote control" parenting by promoting two-way communication. Children who feel "heard" and the adults who can "hear" them share a deep sense of trust and intimacy that lessens conflict from infancy, through toddlerhood, and well beyond.

3. The History of Baby Signing

In the late **1980**s, **Joseph Garcia**, a student at the University of Alaska, became fascinated with sign language. While there were no deaf people in his family, he thought that learning how to sign would be interesting, and he began to study it seriously.

Once he had a solid grasp of **American Sign Language** (ASL), Garcia made a number of friends in the deaf community. This resulted in an observation that changed his life and the lives of many to come. What Joseph Garcia noticed was that the **hearing babies of his deaf friends** were on their way to becoming sign language "experts" at around 9 months of age. Yet, the **9-month old** babies of his hearing friends were not communicating much at all. The difference intrigued Garcia so much that he made it the subject of his Master's thesis.

Why was it possible, he asked, for deaf babies of that age to communicate by gesturing but hearing babies of the same age unable to communicate at all?

And if deaf parents could communicate with their hearing babies, would there be any benefit to teaching sign language to the hearing children of hearing parents? Using his infant sons as "test subjects," Garcia was able to demonstrate the positive effects of signing with hearing babies in his the-

> **ASL = American Sign Language**
>
> ASL isn't related to English, although it borrows from English — as many spoken languages do.
>
> ASL has its own grammar and syntax.
>
> ASL has word order that's different from English, and it has its own idioms, jokes, and poetry.

sis. Eventually, it evolved into his popular program, "Sign with Your Baby." We'll discuss the benefits of his program later in this module.

The Women's Perspective...

Around the same time, **Linda Acredolo, a PhD** at the University of California at Davis, took her **12-month-old daughter** Kate to the pediatrician. While they were in the waiting room, Kate walked up to the fish tank to get a closer look. And then she did something strange. She started to blow! Her mother was puzzled by the behavior and, after the appointment, took Kate home for a nap. As she put her down in her crib, Linda "activated" the mobile that hung over it. It was a mobile made of beautiful fish, and in order to make them "swim," Linda had to blow on it. Instantly, Linda became **aware of the connection** her daughter had made. Without any instruction, her daughter was communicating with her own form of sign language.

Linda began to wonder: how many other gestures or signs was Kate using to communicate? Were there any other signs that she was making that Linda just hadn't noticed? Do other children try to communicate by gesturing or signing?

And so her quest began. Linda partnered with her colleague, **Susan Goodwyn**, another PhD at the same university, and they began to **study**, observe and question other parents. As scientists, they did things right. With a grant from the **National Institutes of Child Health and Human Development**, they compared babies who signed with babies who didn't. They followed their progress at ages 2, 3 and 8 and got remarkable results! Acredolo and Goodwyn's findings were nothing short of **extraordinary**. They proved conclusively that once babies are taught to sign, their brains become more developed, resulting in one positive benefit after another. In comparison after comparison, signers out-performed non-signers in all areas.

4. When to Start Signing?

When should I start signing with my baby? A quick browse on the net will result in various answers, no surprise, and the truth is that I do not like to give an exact time frame to any parent. Children are unique in their development, and sign language is no different than rolling over, sitting up, smiling, crawling, and walking. Your baby will sign according to his/her own time frame.

> **FYI**
> Baby Sign Language and Baby Signing are based on ASL.
> Baby Signs are based on ASL but also have some made-up compromised signs.

Babies are often ready to sign back when they sit by themselves and can point. Does that mean we should only start signing at that time? Definitely not! We start talking to them well before this point, and the same applies to sign language. In fact, babies who are born to families with deaf parents or siblings are exposed to signing at birth. There is no 'too young' or 'too old' ~ you are the expert on your child, and your instincts will lead the way. Keep in mind, however, that babies are fast learners and may understand what you are signing well before they are able to sign back.

Recently, I received an e-mail from Magda, a mom who uses sign language after participating in our class. Her message read: "I took Etel's class when my son was 5 months. By 6 months, he started signing 'milk', wow. My son was fascinated by the class, looking at everybody signing at the same time."

5. Benefits to Signing with Babies and Toddlers

Benefits for Babies:
- Able to easily express needs.
- Feel less frustrated.
- Spend less time crying.
- Bond with parents.
- Improve linguistic development
- Verbal language:
    » Baba- Bottle / Bubble / Balloon / Bath
- Concepts:
    » Hurt, Help, Medicine

- Enhance self esteem.
- Reinforce Memory.
- Develop creative skills.
- Receive intellectual stimulation.
- Learn the most important skill for a lifetime:
- Communication!

Benefits for Toddlers:

- Less "terrible twos."
- Don't bite out of frustration.
- Larger vocabularies
- By age 2, 50 more spoken words
- By age 3, age 4 learning level
- Improved IQ scores.
- Better imagination.
- Greater interest in books.
- Better spellers.
- More productively expressed emotion.
- Manners learned in early age.
- More interactivity with peers.
- Culturally sensitivity.
- Communication outside their native language group.
- Facilitated 2nd language learning.
- Benefits for Parents:
- Better bond with their child

- No 'guessing game':
  - » Wet diaper?
  - » Hungry?
  - » Sick?
  - » Need some TLC?
- Scared from noise?
- Less dealing with "terrible twos".
- Window to the child's mind and thoughts.
- Communication in loud places.
- Opportunity to just have FUN!

Benefits for Educators:

- Reduced noise levels in classrooms.
- Minimized stress and frustration for both children and staff.
- Significantly reduced aggressive behavior, including a great impact on biting problems.
- Demonstration of the fact that childcare facility actively participates in the child's development.
- Accelerated development of verbal language
- Improved integration amongst diverse populations.

Chapter Two:
Let's Start: Tips and Tools

1. Twelve Simple Steps to Signing

1. Begin with the Basics

It is best to start with meaningful signs that you feel are important for your baby. It is highly recommended to start with tangible objects that your child sees often (not concepts!!) such as: "MILK" and "MOM" or "DAD" and "BALL." Do not start with the sign "MORE"; it is a concept.

2. Keep Concepts until Later

Introduce concepts only after your child recognizes at least three signs. Concepts such as MORE should not be taught as first signs as they can be confusing to your child and are easily replaced by pointing or a cry.

3. Say the Words as You Sign

Remember, signing doesn't come instead of speaking; it is a tool for communication. It is important to engage with your child verbally while signing. Sign *important* words as you speak. For example: "Are you HUNGRY", "Do you want MILK," or "WHERE is MOMMY?" or "DADDY is here."

4. Make Eye Contact

One of the key elements in signing with your child is eye contact. Make sure you make eye contact with your child as you're signing so that your child will feel connected and empowered.

5. Exaggerate on Motion

Babies tend to focus on motion. The movement of your signs will capture your baby's attention. To help your baby learn the sign faster, repeat beginner's signs often in an exaggerated motion. At first it will seem strange and funny, but soon signing will become part of your routine and part of your communication.

6. Repeat, Repeat, Repeat

The more your child is exposed to signing, the easier it will be for your baby to learn and remember the signs.

7. Include Everyone

The more the merrier. To help reinforce learning, invite family members, caregivers, childcare providers, and friends to sign with you. Make play dates with friends who sign with their children.

8. Do Not Give Up Too Early

Keep signing even if your child doesn't sign back. Sometimes it takes time. Do not miss out on the wonderful opportunity to enjoy your child's thoughts and desires while he communicates with you. A child's first sign is simply magical.

9. Engage Daily Routine

You don't have to make time for signing; signing happens as you communicate with your child during daily routine activities such as meal time, play time, bath time, and bed time. To keep it simple, ensure your signs reflect daily routines.

10. Celebrate Your Child's Signing

When you communicate with your baby and he/she signs back to you, celebrate and cheer him/her! Ensure and acknowledge your child's efforts to motivate him/her to continue using signs.

11. Leave Space for Approximation

Some signs (like the sign DOG) require several hand movements. Accept your child's approximation. At this point, your child is in the 'baby talk' stage of signing. It is a great step toward communication, and it signifies your baby is learning the concept of signing. Continue to show the correct sign, but do not correct your baby. Repetition will help your baby to learn the how to properly form the right sign.

12. Smile

Make sure you have lots of laughs and giggles along your signing journey. This is a great opportunity to bond and connect with your baby during meaningful daily interactions.

2. First Five Tips
for Beginning Signers

Use the acronym **SS ROC** to remember these tips. (It's easy to remember because **SS ROC** stands for **SignShine® Rocks!**)

1. **Start** with 3-6 signs (These will get you started.).
2. **Speak** as you sign.
3. **Repeat** and be consistent.
4. Sign for different **Opportunities**:
   » Mealtime, Play time, Story time, etc.
5. Remain **Committed**!

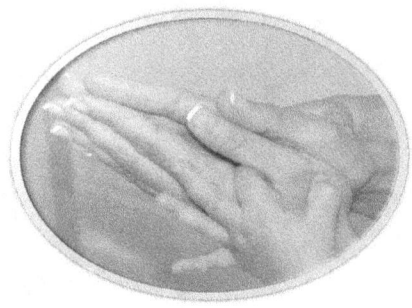

3. Five Stages of Baby Signing

Use the Acronym **STAGES** to follow your child's five stages of signing:

Stares & **S**miles
Try
Attempt
Generate First Signs
Enjoy and...**S**mile

Stares & Smiles

At first your baby will stare at you when you sign with him/her. Your child will find your movements amusing and will smile at you. You might even feel funny and uncomfortable at first. This is very natural. During this stage, keep signing and most importantly make eye contact.

Try

Your baby will show more interest in your signs. Your child makes the association and the connections between the verbal word, the object, and the sign. For example, a book. S/he will see a book, hear the word *book*, and watch you signing BOOK. Your baby will try to imitate your hand movements by playing with his/her own fingers and hands. Do not underestimate these little moves; your child is mimicking you and exploring fine motor skills.

Attempt

Your baby will attempt to make his/her first sign. It might be so random that you will not even notice. Do not question the first sign. If you think it is a sign, it is a sign. Just like babbling *mama* for mommy for the first time. Praise, give positive reinforcement, and repeat. First signs may not look correct at first; this is common. In Baby Signing, we call this *approximation*. Keep signing without correcting. Some children also sign the same sign for many words.

Signing "crocodile" with Zoë.

Generate First Signs

Reinforce your child's understanding as s/he signs and you introduce more signs; your baby will soon make his or her first sign. This time, you will be sure signing is part of the communication. This is the magical part of communicating with your baby, personally, my favorite stage. You and your child will enjoy such a special connection every time you sign.

Enjoy & Smile

Your baby now understands the concept of signing and often asks for things or shows you things using signs. Take a pen and a little notebook or open a file on your computer, and start journaling your child's signs. Soon, you will be amazed how many signs s/he knows. Your baby will look at you and smile and sign away. At this point, your family is fully engaged in signing and enjoys an amazing way of communicating with each other.

> Language comes from the LEFT side of the brain. Sign Language comes from the LEFT and RIGHT sides of the brain, since it is visual language.

Please be aware that these stages are merely a suggestion and not meant to suggest that your child will follow these steps in this exact order. It is common for children to skip or replace expected steps in different orders.

4. Face-to-Face Time

As parents, we go to great lengths to provide our kids with the best life experience. We have stacks of parenting books next to our beds, we take endless pictures to remember all the "firsts," we find interesting activities and friends, we expose them to culture, books, new places, etc. This is all in addition to the endless basic care we give them. But at the end of the day, we should all keep in mind that parenting is really about building a relationship with our children. A positive and healthy parental relationship is what makes our children feel safe, loved, and able to function successfully in the world. And at the very heart of any healthy relationship, we find good communication.

The latest research shows us that the basis for building a healthy relationship with your child is face-to-face time (Strasburger, 2007). Babies require face-to-face interactions to learn. The new study by Zimmerman and Christakis suggests that children who were read to or had storytelling time with their parents showed an increase in language skills.

Signing with your child offers an excellent opportunity for face-to-face time. After all, signing is not possible unless you and your child are facing each other and making eye contact. "Every interaction with your child is meaningful," says Christakis. "Time is precious in those early years, and the newborn is watching you, and learning from everything you do."

Ideas for face-to-face time with your child:

- React to the grimaces and giggles.
- Mimic their sounds.
- Extrapolate from 'bababa' to bottle.
- Label and sign things they touch and see.
- Read and sign their favorite book.
- Sing and sign children's rhymes.
- Play hide and seek with signing.
- Respond to their cues as they talk to you.

Each country has its own sign language.
For example:

Hebrew Sign Language
French Sign Language
British Sign Language
German Sign Language

Some say there are 200 different Sign Languages in the world.

Chapter Three:
Beyond MILK and BABY

1. Family Business: Signs of Love

"From the moment Eli was born, the bond between my wife and my son was so special I felt left out. I love my little boy, but it's harder for me to connect with him than it is for my wife. Monique breastfed Eli, they have their own language, she understands his cries. When she tells me he's hungry, or he's tired, I wonder how she knows that, when I'm just completely confused. Will I have to wait until Eli is old enough to talk and play boy games with me to really bond with him?"

ASL IS A GREAT TOOL for deepening familial connections. Fathers especially often tell me they're waiting for their kids to talk to them to experience the deep bonds they witness between their kids and their wives. Because teaching children ASL allows them to communicate clearly with adults even before they can vocalize or verbalize clearly, signing together can help fathers feel they're "catching up" on the intimacy they witness between their wives and their children much sooner than they had supposed.

Signing together encourages sibling bonding, as well because signing is a two-way activity that older children actually enjoy sharing with their younger brothers and sisters. Not only do older kids enjoy teaching their younger siblings, they also enjoy the sense of connection that sharing a common language creates with one another. The power of communication goes a long way towards easing conflict and resentment among children just as it lessens power struggles between children and adults.

> "When I was a child, I knew all of my cousins. We lived in the same town. We saw each other at least once a week and were very close. But now that we're all grown up and living far from each other, it seems my two kids know my girlfriend's kids better than Benjamin and Ian, my sister's kids. I wish I can change that, and explain what cousins are without confusing them."

ASL is great for creating a bond with family members who are far away. My own kids have six cousins in Israel, and our family is always looking for ways to create connections with our relatives overseas. One way we do that is by teaching the signs for relatives like grandparents, aunts, uncles, and cousins. We create nicknames for those relatives, too, so that they have a presence in our home, even when they're not there.

This is why I encourage parents to try to involve aunts, uncles, grandparents, older siblings, and other relatives—because it offers a shorthand and quick connection when visits are shor, or few and far between. Often, I hear complaints that a grandparent or a cousin isn't enthusiastic about signing with children because they believe it will stall verbal development or because they believe signing is some sort of silly fad. Don't waste time trying to change their minds. Your signing child will do that for them. The first time your judgmental sister witnesses your daughter calmly sign *"HELP"* or your son flash *"I LOVE YOU"* across the room, she'll come around.

Making placemats of family members who are far away, keeps them close.

An example of a placemat for signing:

Make a placemat with your child's favorite toys, family members, or favorite color. (Our example placemat is in blue.)

As your child eats, you can sign the signs in the placemat.

You can ask your child to find the items you sign on the placemat.

Example of a DIY Placemat:

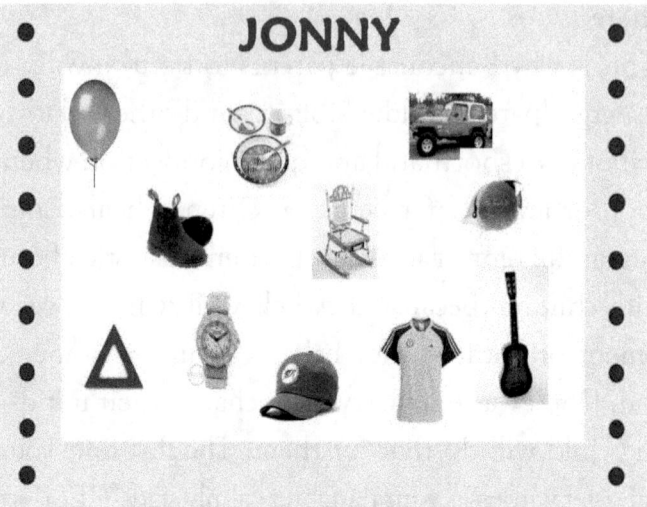

2. Signing in Bilingual Settings
Bridging the Language Gap:
ASL in Bilingual Homes:

"Growing up in Brazil, I assumed my own kids would speak Portuguese. I married a man who spoke Portuguese, and so continued to assume we'd pass it on to our kids. But here in the States, it's just so much easier to speak English as our primary language, because that's the language of most of our friends. For a while, I tried speaking both languages with our daughter, constantly translating what

I said in Portuguese into English, and the reverse. But I worried she couldn't understand me, and it was really hard to keep it up. Now I've largely stopped trying, and I feel awful about it. I worry my daughter will not just lose the language of her parents, but her connection to her relatives in Brazil who speak that language, as well as the cultures and traditions that are rightfully hers."

My own home is quadrilingual. My first language is Hebrew while my husband and children's is English. Our nanny is a native Spanish speaker. I knew early in my first pregnancy that I wanted my children to benefit from all these languages, but until I discovered signing, I wasn't sure how to integrate so many different vocabularies without causing confusion in our home.

Signing became a common language for everyone in our household because it was an easy way to express synonyms across languages. Whether I offered my daughter **chalav**, her nanny handed her **leche** or my husband poured her a bottle of **milk**, we all used the same ASL sign to describe it. In this way, it was easy for my kids to learn new words across language barriers because the sign we used was always the same.

Signing as a multiple-language tool is a wonderful way to impress upon our children the essential similarities among people and races all over the world. In this way, signing encourages tolerance. Signing is a way to make the unknown familiar, and it teaches our kids the most important skill in the world: understanding.

"We are an American family living in Los Angeles. We only speak English at home. This is such an international city that most of our friends are raising bilingual kids, teaching them the languages from the countries of their birth – Spanish, French, German, and Hebrew! We worry that Maya will be at a disadvantage when she goes to school, knowing only one language, when so many of her peers know two. We have been thinking about hiring a Spanish-speaking caregiver for Maya, to expose her to Spanish. We've considered ASL as another alternative–but is that really considered a second language?"

Even if your house isn't inherently bilingual, ASL is a great way to introduce the concept of multiple languages to your child. ASL is the 3rd most used language among 322 languages spoken in the United States. With a deaf and hard of hearing population estimated at close to 8 million individuals by the US Census Bureau, not to mention family members who may hear but still need to communicate with them, some estimate the ASL-using population to be as high as 20 million.

Teaching your child ASL is also a proven way to begin to hardwire the ability to learn a second language in your child's young brain. We have long known that it is easier to learn a second language as a small child while the pathways of the brain are still being mapped. Studies now suggest that a child who has learned a second language early in life has an easier time learning even more languages as they age because their brains already know how. Signing can be your child's "gateway" second language.

HANDS ON!: If you do not speak another language at home, introduce your child to his favorite sign in a different language. Try to use a language your child is likely to hear in your area. The internet is a fabulous resource for learning simple vocabulary in any language you can imagine!

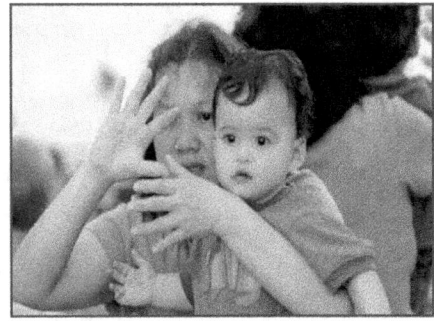

3. Teaching Manners

We all share the goal of raising children who are well-mannered, kind, and perhaps can even share their toys without too much protest! Teaching gratitude starts from a very early age, but it can be a difficult endeavor. For example, many parents struggle between the desire to give their children everything and the knowledge that kids won't get far in life with a sense of entitlement unaccompanied by good manners. Teaching gratitude happens most effectively in the simple moments when we are thankful for the intangible.

My daughter Zoë learned to sign PLEASE at 13 months. When she began to speak, she still signed and said PLEASE when she really wanted something. Somehow, she understood that signing AND speaking had more of an impact. I'm sure that you, too, can teach your child these important signs that will serve as a great foundation for good manners.

Emphasizing manners through sign language with babies and children teaches etiquette from a young age, and it becomes a natural part of the way they interact with people. It gives visual support to remind our little ones to be kind and also makes it fun.

Signing is very effective in teaching gratitude, a common concept all parents hope their child will learn. Teaching gratitude starts from a very early age, but it can be a difficult endeavor. Manners are an abstract concept, but kids will catch on when they watch you end every request by signing PLEASE. When your child hands you his or her toy, respond by signing and saying THANK YOU; it will become a habit and will make a difference in the long run.

Teaching gratitude happens most effectively in the simple moments when we are thankful for the intangible objects. Emphasizing manners through sign language with babies and children teaches etiquette from a young age, and it becomes a natural part of the way they interact with people. Teaching manners with sign provides visual support to remind our little ones, in a fun way, to be kind.

Manners to Start With:

- Meet and greet others:
- Hello & Good Bye.
- Behave in public places:
- Share, My Turn, Your Turn, and Excuse Me.
- Improve table manners:
- May I Be Excused, Thank You, Please.
- Develop social skills:
- Share, Take Turns, Please, Sorry, Friend.

Chapter Four: Let's Play

1. Signing Games and Activities

Children (and adults) learn while playing; it is most natural and enjoyable to acquire new ideas by incorporating fun games into the process of learning sign language. The following games can be used as an effective reinforcement tool to teach your baby new signs, bond with your child, and create moments of connection between the two of you, all while having fun.

Hide and Seek Dolly Body Object Performance

This game is based Jean Piaget's **Body Object Permanence,** a study of infants based on their ability to realize that an object exists even when it is not in sight. When babies develop object permanence, they are ready for language and are able to assign a label or word to an object. Hide your baby's favorite toy and ask "Where is _____ (car, ball, doll, teddy, etc.)?" Match the hiding place with your baby's age. For younger babies, simply put it under a sheer fabric right next to him/her. As s/he grows, place the item under a toy-bucket, but show it to your baby first.

Peek-a-Boo! Where is Mommy/ Daddy?

Cover your head with a sheer fabric, and say: "BYE ____ (name)," Now ask: "WHERE is MOMMY?"— and sign Where and MOMMY or DADDY. Then pop in, and say "Peek-a-boo! Here is MOMMY or DADDY." Another version is covering your child's face with the fabric (Make sure it is a breathable, sheer fabric.). Ask the same questions.

With older kids, you can actually hide behind an object. Then, run into the room signing MOMMY or DADDY, as you say the words "Here's MOMMY or DADDY." Give many kisses as you both laugh and giggle.

Bath Time Fun

Introduce bath and body signs. Turn bath time into a fun song; as you wash your child, teach them their body parts. Try the children's song, "Head, shoulders, knees and toes, knees and toes." You clearly show your child eyes, head, mouth, nose, etc. while singing the song. You can use a plastic doll, dog, bear, or other 'friend' to have children point to eye, mouth, and nose.

Concentration Signing

This game helps to develop memory. Cut out two of each picture of familiar objects that you and baby have been practicing. Lay all the cards upside down. Then, select one card, and turn it over and look at the picture. Sign and say the name of the picture. Now, find the match. This game is an ideal way to reinforce signs. Eventually, your baby can discover the pairs alone.

Identify Animals

Find pictures of your favorite animals, and cover the picture of the animal, asking your child where it is: "WHERE is the Dog?" Let your child uncover the animal to find it (or find it for her). Sign, "WHERE is the MONKEY?" You can sing Old Mac Donald and sign as you point to the animal. Uncover the animal picture, and praise your child's find, saying and signing, "You found the MONKEY!" Increase your baby's attention span by hiding multiple pictures at once.

Emotions and Feelings

Emotions and feelings are a complex concept. To start teaching feelings, I love using books, magazine, and pictures of other babies as babies love other babies. First, identify the feeling: "The BABY is HAPPY," or "The BABY is CRYING; he is SAD." Teach your baby how to effectively express their feelings and wants in a fun way. Feelings of frustration result from the inability to communicate. By identifying other babies' feelings, you show your child and teach him/her to let you know if s/he are hurt, sad, and sick.

Silly Hurt

Teaching the sign HURT can be done in a silly way. Pretend you hurt yourself on your knee. Pretend you're crying (in a silly way), and sign HURT over your knee. This is a great tool when your child hurts or is sick. You can ask, "Where does it HURT?" while signing "HURT" by your ear, mouth, tummy, or knee.

Books, Magazines, & Your Own Sign Language Book

Review your favorite books. A few of my favorites are books with repetitive sentences (like *Brown Bear* by Eric

Carl). Baby, mothering, and parenting magazines contain several pictures of babies performing daily routines that you can explain to your baby (Babies love baby pictures.). You can say and sign, "EAT BANANA," "BABY is SLEEPING," "DRINK MILK", "PLAY with the BALL," etc. You can also make your own book; simply add your favorite pictures. You can even make your own flashcards with your child's pictures. Every time you come across a familiar word, sign it as you read.

Signing "music" with Zoë

Sing and Sign the Hello Song

Use the hello song to identify familiar objects or teach new ones. Turn identifying household objects into a game. As you walk around the house, sing and sign "HELLO and object name!" For example, identify the puppy and sign and say, "HELLO PUPPY" Have fun! "HELLO MOMMY," "HELLO APPLE."

Big, Small and other Opposites

Opposites are another concept which can be taught easily with signing. SMALL and BIG: take a bucket or a pan from the kitchen. Bring two balls, one that is SMALL and one BIG. Place it inside the bucket and sign, "SMALL BALL." Ask your child to do the same; then describe what s/he does. Now take the bigger ball and show your child how it does not fit inside the bucket; sign "BIG BALL." Show your child how one fits INSIDE and the other doesn't; sign BIG and SMALL. Repeat with other toys like cars or blocks - and have fun with it.

Try this game for other opposites such as SLOW and FAST. Sign FAST and SLOW as you play, run, dance. My favorite way to teach SLOW and FAST is by simply looking at the washing machine together.

Collect various boxes, and practice opening and closing the boxes with your baby, thus practicing the fine motor skills. Sign CLOSE and OPEN.

Find the Treasure

Now that your child knows the signs for OPEN and CLOSE, you can play WHAT IS INSIDE? Choose a few objects that your child already knows the sign for (or even produce the sign) and put them inside the box. Ask, "What is INSIDE the BOX?" Let your child open the box. See his face light up when he opens the box. You can sign the item/toy together.

For even more fun - leave some boxes empty to practice: WHERE–WHERE is the _____ (toy)? Let your child discover which box contains the object. During Easter season, I highly recommend purchasing colorful plastic eggs for play throughout the year. Your child will love figuring out how to open the egg to discover the object inside.

The Concept of More

When your child is eating or having fun ask your child if s/he wants more? Sign "MORE" as you give your child more of what s/he wants. It is easy for children to catch on to the idea of *more* and sign MORE on their own. Use the concept of *more* to reinforce other signs that your baby is learning. Remember, you want to expose your child to the sign MORE, only after s/he understands the concept of signing.

Mirror Mirror

Choose special signs; as you see the sign in reflection, say word. Try facial expressions and movements also. Try pointing and signing in front of a mirror. If your child's favorite toy is a car, hold the car in front of the mirror, and say *car* as you sign CAR. Once you get your baby's attention, let him/her focus on reflection, and show him/her the sign of the object. If your child signs, wait for him/her to sign back to you.

Music Instruments

Use signs to teach your baby the sound of music. A guitar goes hum, a drum goes boom, a flute whistles, etc. Sign the instrument, and sign the sound. Make music instruments from simple objects in your home if you do not own your own instruments: you can always create drums from kitchen containers. Children love creativity. Sign, MUSIC and SONGS. You can make up a simple song signing your child's name and finger spell the letters of his/her name.

2. Ten Ideas and Activities to Promote Verbal Communication

Signing is **one of the best** tools to build speech and language development while providing an excellent bonding experience with children. As mentioned throughout this book, signing with your baby is an excellent way to bridge the gap between comprehension and speech production. Use of a few daily routines can strengthen your baby's understanding. Make the experience a fun one to remember.

Even if your baby isn't old enough to understand some of these concepts, repetition will help them learn!

1. Voice tone

Studies show that babies favor high pitched voices, that "baby voice" that adults tend to use naturally when speaking to babies. (However, avoid baby talk!)

2. Vowel-like and consonant-vowel

Encourage your baby to make sounds such as "ma," "da," and "ba" by making a game of it. Imitate your baby's words, and then see if s/he will imitate some of yours.

3. Eye contact is key

After getting your child's attention, **respond** to attempts to speak.

4. Imitate

Either imitate or teach to imitate. Copy your baby's **laughter and facial expressions**. Then, perform actions that your baby can mimic: clapping, kisses, and finger games such as itsy-bitsy-spider.

5. Speak often

Talk as you perform daily routines. (Form signs with words whenever necessary.) Talk about what you are doing, where you are going, what you will do when you arrive, and who/what you will see.

6. Identify concepts

Asking for HELP, expressing PAIN, requesting MORE, expressing feelings, and counting are concepts that your child can identify easily with signing. Practice these concepts when performing daily routines after you've already exposed your child to other tangible signs. For example, when you feed your baby, ask him/her if s/he wants more. During dress time, ask baby to count their shoes; say, "count one, two shoes!" Sign the words to the concepts as you talk.

7. Associate, Acknowledge, and Ask

Match sounds to a specific meaning. For example, "The dog says woof woof." **Associate the object to the concept,** i.e. a concept of speech: "Woof." **Acknowledge any response;** then, **ask questions** to reinforce concepts. If your child is unsure how to respond, always identify the answer for your little one.

8. Increase Vocabulary

Use **single words** that your baby already knows in new sentences. For instance, "Here is the DOG," "The DOG is sleeping," "The DOG barks woof-woof," or "Where is the DOG?"

9. Read Often

Choose beginner books, and sign a few words. As your baby learns the stories, ask **questions to strengthen your baby's understanding.** You can start with a simple question as "Where is [say and sign]?" looking for the object in the illustration. Next time you read the same book, you can just sign the object: "Where is [sign only]? Remember children love repetition and will love to read the same book over and over again.

10. Use proper language

Avoid baby talk, by all means. You want your child to learn proper language; therefore, speak to your child in **complete sentences and use proper pronunciation.**

3. Teaching the Concept "More": MORE is Not the First Sign

Most parents believe the common approach to learning sign is to teach "MORE" as one of the first signs. In contrast to this approach and from years of experience, I highly recommend not to start with the sign MORE because it is a concept rather than a tangible object and can be replaced by a cry or "I want this" or "I want that." That is exactly the sign that will discourage communication. After all MORE can be used as MORE play, MORE water, MORE grapes, thus eliminating the need for child to learn actual object names as they think they simply need to say "more." The goal of signing is to encourage specific and precise descriptions; therefore, teach your baby object names before MORE. Introduce the sign MORE only after your child was exposed to other signs and can recognize at least three other signs and can even produce signs on their own.

MORE likes MORE Signs

When you are ready to introduce the sign MORE, make sure you always sign and say with other signs your child knows. If he knows MILK, say and sign "MORE MILK?" If she signs WATER, say and sign: "MORE WATER?" It is important not to sign MORE by itself, at least in the first stage of signing.

4. More Bubbles and Creative MORE

Bubbles are a fun and creative way to teach the concept MORE. Blowing bubbles are a visual form of the concept MORE and allows children to be active participants in the process. Children can watch them, catch them, and blow bubbles themselves. Blowing bubbles is an amazing tool to improve language development.

8 Benefits for Blowing Bubbles with your Child:

- Encourages eye contact.
- Encourages hand-eye coordination.
- Encourages children to make a request:
  » MORE, STOP, and FAST.
- Encourages making the primer sound 'B'.

- Encourages tongue strengthening and speech development.
- Encourages signing of signs such as ALL DONE or WHERE.
- Encourages play time in many different places: room, outdoor, bath time, and in the park.
- Encourages FUN and moments of bonding.

You can make or buy your bubbles; you can even add coloring to your bubbles for extra fun. Once your baby grows s/he will love a variety of colored bubbles.

Use colored bubbles as an educational tool to introduce all the colors. (This can be messy so it's best as an outside activity.) For various bubble types, follow these directions:

Basic Bubbles

- 2 Ts dish soap
- 1 c water

Color Bubbles

- 1 c liquid Tempera paints
- 2 Ts dish detergent
- 1 Ts liquid starch

Magic Bubbles

- 1 Ts glycerin
- 2 Ts dish soap
- 9 oz water

Tips for Bubbly Success

1. Get down to the child's level

Start by blowing the bubbles as your baby stares in amazement. Say while signing, "Look at all the BUBBLES!" Blow the bubbles again and again.

2. Make eye contact with your baby

After bubbles pop, look at your baby and ask, "Would you like some MORE BUBBLES? MORE?" (Remember your facial expressions!)

3. Say the word as you sign

"Would you like some MORE BUBBLES? MORE?" To teach your baby more concepts, you can expand with other signs such as FINISHED, ALL DONE, and WHERE are the BUBBLES?

4. Form the sign in their sight line

Pull out the bubbles. Blow some; then stop. Look the child in the eye, and sign "Do you want some MORE?" Remember to form the signs where they can see them.

5. Encourage them!

As your baby grows, encourage your child to blow bubbles; s/he will love it and will feel so empowered.

Chapter Five:
From Signs to Words:
Literacy Skills and Signing

SIGNING WITH YOUR CHILD WILL not only empower communication between the both of you, but it also enhances literacy skills, enriches language, builds vocabulary, and prepares a strong foundation for your little reader. How? Simply by reading and signing books.

> "I really don't want to pressure Ben, but I feel that he needs to know the ABCs already. He is almost two. How can I show him a fun way to learn it? Should I buy booklets? We have puzzles, we sing songs – I want him to have fun! He is just a child."

Parents often feel they need to bombard their child with learning activities but worry that their child will not have enough playtime or fun. Signing is a great way to emphasize fun without skimping on the learning. In fact, research by Dr. Linda Acredolo shows that signing with children, an essentially fun activity, can improve their IQ by up to 12 points!

One of the reasons signing is a great teaching tool is that it allows you to repeat and review the words you speak. Signing is a method of instruction similar to what your child might experience in school when his teacher asks him to rephrase a statement or assignment in his own words to ensure understanding.

Signing is a fantastic way to teach the alphabet because each distinct letter you sign while chanting the alphabet emphasizes that it is a distinct symbol and not just part of a larger, amorphous chain of noise. You can sign the alphabet with children before they have the power of speech and show them how letters of the alphabet can be used to signify names of people and places. For instance, you can show your child the letters of her name, simultaneously speaking, reading, and signing those letters to her. Doing this teaches the concept of letters of the alphabet used to build words and language, so babies can identify names.

1. Use Signing to Emphasize Learning:

Signing the alphabet - finger spelling while teaching ABCs emphasizes letters of the alphabet, people, places, or words without ASL signs.

Read with your child - if you sign while reading, you are constantly underlining the characters and action you are narrating, deepening your child's understanding of the books.

Signing and singing - if you sign what you sing, you are adding another layer of emphasis to the song and helping your child to understand the words you sing.

Signs are also an easy way to teach complicated concepts like synonyms. For instance, if you often sing and sign "Row Row Row Your Boat" *and* "You are My Sunshine" with your child, you will notice that the sign for "Merrily" in the first song and "Happy" in the second are the same. Your child will notice, too, thus easily absorbing those two words can share the same meaning.

Signs are a useful way to teach opposites, prepositions, colors, and adjectives.

2. Reasons to Sign with Books

Now that you and baby have signed for a while, start signing more with books. Remember to start with simple repetitive books. Don't try to sign every word; start with the basics; sign words that are used in daily routine so that your child can begin to recognize these objects.

Signing with books ...

- Promotes the opportunity for your child to be an active participant in reading. S/he feels involved when s/he signs along to the book as you read.
- Builds and strengthens literacy skills and understanding of language.
- Develops the imagination of both the child and the parent.
- Promotes meaning of words and captures your child's attention.
- Associates reading with positive experiences.
- Creates opportunities for interaction, socialization, and parent/child bonding - get the whole family involved for family bonding!

3. How to Sign with Books

Focus on the picture. Share the sign for the picture as you say the word.

Keep eye contact and produce sign word in the baby's line of vision, keeping hand shapes where s/he can see as s/he is drawn to the motion. This may mean signing in front of the book or on the baby if necessary.

Let your child take charge. If s/he skips pages or turns to the same page over and over, sign the words from that page as you say them repeatedly. Watch for baby's attempts to sign!

FYI: Many signs in ASL have Regional Signs. For example, there are about 10 different signs for Happy Birthday.

Use your child's eye contact as an opportunity to gain attention so that your baby can focus on the sign as you read from the book, AS YOU SAY THE WORDS ALWAYS!

4. Opportunities to Sign with Books

Signing with books builds and strengthens literacy skills, creates understanding of language, and associates reading with positive experiences. Here are a few of my favorite tips when signing with books, but don't stop there you can make many more of your own!

1) Story Time

During story time, which is an important part of your baby's learning, position your baby on your lap and place the book on a pillow in front of or beside your baby. As you read the words, sign in front of your baby with your arms around them; sign on their body (for example, sign TEDDY with your hands on their shoulder) or sign right on top of the picture in the book (for example, FISH).

2) Play time

Position your baby facing you in a bouncy seat, highchair, or propped up with pillows (This is the best position with babies that do not sit by themselves yet.). This way, your child sees your facial expressions, hands, and the book all at the same time, and you can see your child, too. You should make eye contact while reading the book. As you read with your baby, say basic words from book, form the sign of the word with your hands in front of your body in exaggerated motion repeatedly, especially new signs.

3) Family Time

Family reading is a great way to bond! Have mommy, daddy, and/or siblings around baby, where baby can see the whole family. Place the book in front of baby, and have a person or people (mommy, daddy, or siblings) sign in front of baby at his/her eye-level. As each family member takes turns reading and signing, make sure they sign the word slowly in an exaggerated motion. This is a great bonding experience, especially for older siblings, who can be the leaders and read a book they already know.

4) Bed Time

Before bed, try nightlight reading. Dim the light behind you, and it will cast a shadow of the sign on the book!

5. Signing with Verbal Children

Why should you continue signing with children when they start to become more verbal?

The beginning of a baby's verbal stage is marked by grunts and other sounds as s/he points to let us know what s/he wants. Slowly, they form words. This is a wonderful phase of development - our little ones are discovering the concept that his or her sounds connect to things and actions. They want to express themselves to tell you what they want, think, feel, and see. This can be a fun but frustrating phase; however, it can be much easier and more of a fun time by using sign language.

Communication is vital to your child, especially when she or he doesn't quite have the verbal skills to say what's on his/her mind. If you're like most parents, you'll find yourself a bit puzzled as you try to interpret these early conversations. For example, when Jonah said, "da da," his parents knew he meant "ALL DONE" because he also used big hand gestures to show the sign for "ALL DONE." If Jonah wouldn't have known how to use that sign, the simple "da da" could have also meant "Daddy" or all kinds of other possibilities. How confusing is that? It's a challenge to make sense of our little ones' great attempt to talk to us - was that "Juice" or "Cheese?" "Ball" or "Bottle?"

"Baby" Sign language is a bit of a misnomer. Many parents and preschool teachers successfully use sign language well into children's toddler and preschool years. This is when the miracles of signing continue. Sign language bridges the gap between a child's ability to understand language, and the ability to articulate it, building on an earlier and more developed language path in the brain.

Many parents ask me about the research related to signing with babies and toddlers. The latest research by Dr. Marilyn Daniels, a professor of communication arts and sciences at Penn State University, finds that signing leads to success in reading, writing, vocabulary, spelling, and memory. You can read more at http://www.marilyndaniels.com/

While early literacy skills and increased intelligence are certainly important, I see these things simply as side benefits. The most important and meaningful benefit is sign language's ability to enrich the parent-child relationship.

Signing increases the number of positive interactions and decreases the number of negative interactions, a formula that naturally leads to a closer relationship. All children - all people for that matter - want to be understood. Sign language makes that possible for our little sweeties; what better gift could we give them?

Chapter Six: Who Else Signs?

1. Caregivers Sign

Often times, the little signers in my SignShine® classes come with their moms. Dads and grandparents are always welcome to come, as well, even if it is for a one-time visit. Many family members have stopped by for a class while visiting from out-of-town. They always have so much fun, and it's a great way to bond with their little loved ones and also to learn about signing.

Another important person within many families is the caregiver/nanny. In our classes, we sometimes have moms bring their nannies with them, and some nannies come on their own with the little ones while the parents are at work. It is amazing to see the special bond created between the child and the nanny.

Harmonie, 17 months old, came regularly to our classes with her nanny, Dawn:

"I am a nanny for 17-month-old Harmonie since she was 3 months old. She is a very bright child. As soon as I started using the basic signs, Harmonie started copying me straight away. Her favorite sign is more. She uses it all the time, 'more breakfast', 'more drink', 'more food', she even combines the signs. We use the eat sign for food, and she signs 'more food'. Harmonies' mommy works. Today she said 'mommy is coming home soon', and she said and signed to me mommy. I was so proud of her that she had used her sign and not only her language and she understood what I was saying. When Harmonie's mommy came home she was thrilled!

Thank you for your great advice, I'm so glad we stuck with it. It's had a positive impact, helping us bond and have fun together." –**Dawn M., Los Angeles, Calif.**

Caregivers create their own unique relationship with the children they take care of, and learning sign language together helps to strengthen that bond. In addition, the child benefits greatly when everyone in their world is signing with them. This is the magic of repetition. Just as you would see with a child learning a foreign language, the more interactions they have with the new language – in this case, sign language – the faster they will pick it up and the more extensive their signing vocabulary will be.

After many requests from nannies, caregivers, and parents alike, we are now offering a special workshop. SignShine® will be partnering with Nurture & Nanny (www.nurtureandnanny.com) to host a Nanny Sign Language Workshop. I encourage you to send your nanny and your child for this wonderful shared experience.

Remember, when it comes to signing, the more the merrier!

2. Educators Sign

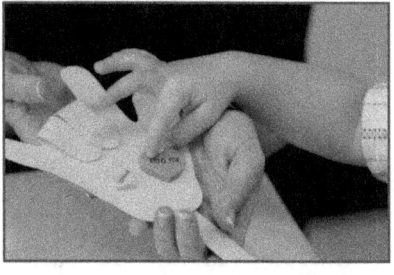

Signing in school settings helps in improving class management, reducing separation anxiety, and decreasing behavioral problems. Signing helps develop positive communication and literacy and social skills and spices up a curriculum in fun and creative ways. You will learn about all the latest research related to sign language in the classroom, obtain helpful resources, and discover how to involve parents in the learning process. Enhance the bond you have with your students as you create a stronger connection through signing.

Teachers are always looking for additional tools to reach young students. Recent studies looked at the benefits and use of sign language in the classroom. Research has found young children who are able to sign and communicate their needs to teachers demonstrate less frustration in the classroom.

The benefits of Teaching Signing in Educational Settings include:

- **Reduced noise levels** in classrooms.
- **Minimized stress and frustration** for children and staff.
- Significantly **reduced aggressive behavior**, i.e. biting.
- Accelerated **development of verbal language.**
- Improved **integration amongst diverse populations.**
- **Encouraged child development.**

3. Signing with Special Needs Children

Children of all abilities can reap the rewards of learning sign language, especially children with special needs. In fact, as parents and professionals who interact with children with special needs know, often the frustration that children can experience is rooted in their difficulty with communicating effectively. Signing is a great way to help your child build a working vocabulary to **assist with communication** and **ease frustration.**

Children with **all types of disabilities,** including autism, Down syndrome, apraxia, speech and language delays, cerebral palsy, and many others, **can benefit** from learning American Sign Language (ASL).

Signing **empowers children** with special needs by offering them a multitude of cognitive, emotional, and social benefits, including:
- Improved communication skills,
- Increased speech and language development.
- Increased confidence and self-esteem,
- Increased social-interactions,
- Reduced negative behaviors.
- More peaceful learning environment.

How Can Signing Help?

Signing can be used **anywhere and everywhere** with **no equipment** needed! Here are just some of the many areas that signing can assist with your child's communication skills:

At home:
- Making requests: eat, drink, more, play, music, all done, sleep.

- Decreasing inappropriate behaviors. (communicating wants and needs, explaining to your child what is going to happen: "time to go to the bathroom").
- During routines (getting dressed, going to bed).
- Expressing pain or sickness.
- Teaching other family members and caregivers (siblings, grandma, grandpa).

In school:

- Communicating with the teacher or aides.
- Expressing learned concepts such as colors, shapes, and numbers.
- Conveying desires (choosing lunch items, a preferred book, or the need for a break).
- Developing peer relationships.
- Decreasing frustration.

In social situations:

- Building peer relationships.
- Requesting items ("my turn", "please").
- Increasing appropriate social behaviors and interactions.
- Providing a communication tool between peers with and without disabilities.

But Wait, I Have Some Questions!

Why should we use sign language if my child is not deaf?

Any child that struggles with spoken language can benefit from using signs. Enhancing communication skills with sign language has a profound impact upon the quality of interactions between children with special needs, their peers, their families, and the professionals who work with them. Sign language is now being used more and more outside the deaf community by children with and without disabilities in order to improve communication.

In fact, **signing is recommended** for children with disabilities for several reasons (Sundberg and Partington, 1998):

Signing is **completely portable** and requires no special equipment.

Signing can be performed at a speed similar to talking.

Signing initiates motor movements, which may **prompt talking**.

Signing may **reduce problem behavior** more effectively because the response form is more efficient than when using picture selection or exchange.

Signing is **easier and quicker to learn** than picture selection or exchange by some children.

Parents or teachers can help a child learn signs by helping mold the child's hand into the correct sign for a given word.

Signing may **enhance receptive language**.

What if my child already uses pictures to communicate?

Great! Finding a successful communication tool for your child can be a challenge, and if pictures are working, you are encouraged to continue using them. Many children with speech and/or language delays use a combination of communication methods. Each child learns differently, and to assume one way or another will fit everyone would be doing a disservice to our children. By adding signs to your child's communication repertoire, either independently or in addition to other forms of communication such as a Picture Exchange Communication System (PECS), a child can have a variety of methods available when his/ her pictures aren't within reach. Signing **requires no extra equipment or materials**, making it possible to communicate wherever you are.

My child is receiving speech and language services. Will learning sign language interfere?

Many parents fear that by learning signs (or another form of communication) their child won't speak. However, according to research, children who learn signs are sometimes even **more motivated to try new words**! By pairing spoken language with signs, a child is being exposed to language both visually and auditorily; signing would not be used in isolation. And often times, as speech begins to emerge, signs can fade. However, they are always there to fall back on when needed!

My child has tantrums. Will signing help?

Many children with speech or language delays can experience frustration when unable to communicate successfully. This frustration can quickly turn into tantruming, crying, or self-injuring behaviors. By giving your child some simple signs to communicate his needs or desires, such as being hungry, being finished with an activity, or wanting to listen to music, his tendency to get upset may very well decrease. Often, the inability to communicate effectively is the root of the frustration, and by alleviating that with sign, **more appropriate behaviors** can surface.

My child has limited motor skills. Is signing still recommended?

Children with disabilities that affect their fine or gross motor skills, such as cerebral palsy, can benefit from signing. While all signs taught are directly from American Sign Language (ASL) vocabulary, as you work with your child to learn, you also learn your child's approximations of the signs. Most children adapt signs to whatever they are physically able to do, so even though some signs may not be exact, the important part is that your child is learning to communicate.

Who Can Use Sign Language?

Children with all types of special needs can benefit from learning ASL including:

- Autism
- Down syndrome
- Apraxia
- Speech and language delays
- Children in hospital settings
- English language learners.

Take a look at how learning sign language can help **your child.**

Signing with Children with Apraxia

Some children with apraxia can become so discouraged by their difficulties speaking that they can stop trying to talk altogether. Research suggests that signing with children with apraxia is meant to be used as **a bridge to learning and using verbal speech** – not a substitute for it.

Signing allows children with apraxia a whole new way to **communicate effectively**, even while learning how to improve speech sounds.

Signing **helps clarify words** that are not yet clearly spoken.

Signing offers children the **confidence** that they will be understood. This confidence can encourage them to learn and practice using more spoken words.

Signing gives a child **visual "cues"** about the words or ideas he is trying to voice.

Signing **slows down the rate of speech**, allowing the child more time to form words or sounds s/he struggles with.

Signing gives children more opportunities to practice their expressive language skills; by using signs, a child can form complete ideas and thoughts for which s/he may not have the speech skills yet.

Signing with Children with Autism

Many children with autism struggle with speech and language as well as social skills. Research suggests that sign language offers children with autism extraordinary communicative, social, and behavioral benefits (Berkell, 1992).

Signing **eases communication** difficulties by offering an alternative method to speech.

Signing has also been shown to **help children learn spoken language** at a faster rate.

Signing **encourages eye contact**.

Signing motivates increased communication. Children can express their needs and wishes in a language that is easily understood and universally accepted.

Signing **improves adaptive behavior** by reducing frustration, crying, tantrums, aggression, and self-injurious behavior.

Signing **improves self-esteem** and self-confidence.

Signing with Children with Down Syndrome

Often, children with Down syndrome struggle with speech and language from an early age; however, a desire to communicate can be strong right from the beginning! By teaching a child sign language, s/he can satisfy that desire when spoken language is developing.

Signing encourages children to **communicate with peers and caregivers** even as they are practicing and perfecting speech skills.

Signing attaches meaning to words by providing a visual representation paired with the sound.

Signing provides children with a means to communicate with their peers, allowing for **more social opportunities**.

Signing **increases self-esteem**.

Signing may be used even after children have overcome speech delays, to provide emphasis for spoken word, or **clarify meanings** when spoken words are difficult for others to understand.

Signing is not a substitute for speech; most vocabulary that children sign will later be spoken aloud.

Signing and Other Special Needs:

Signing with children in hospital settings can provide them with a means of communication when verbal speech is not an option.

Signing with English language learners gives children a visual representation of the words they are learning as well as a tool to communicate with others who speak English.

Chapter Seven: Ask

1. Why Choose Baby Signing?
Mommy & Me Style

The baby signing world has grown tremendously in the last few years. There are books, DVDs, and a lot of information online. Now, that you are impressed by this wonderful world, you might make the next step: take a baby signing class. If your area offers mommy & me style baby signing classes, take the step to join a class; it is an excellent way to empower communication with your child. I highly recommend it for parents, caregivers, and educators.

Benefits of Baby Signing Mommy & Me:

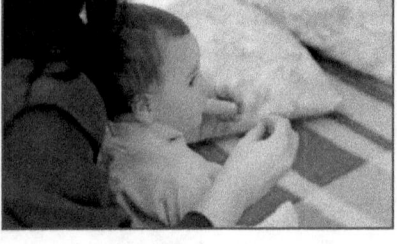

- Bond with your child.
- Laugh with your child.
- Create meaningful interactions.
- Stimulate your baby's brain.
- Decrease moments of crying.
- Be a much more peaceful parent.
- Be amazed by your child.
- Increase more family time/
- See your child tell you what he wants/ feels.
- Stimulate cognitive development.

Why Take a Sign Language Mommy & Me Class?

- You will meet other families who sign.
- You will be exposed to the exact ASL signs.
- You and your baby will enjoy weekly stimulating classes.
- You will learn songs and games you can review and enjoy at home.
- Your child will be able to see other adults and babies sign.

- You will feel empowered.
- You will enjoy a support of professional instructor, who is savvy in both child development and signing.

2. Questions Everyone Asks

How many signs should I be showing my baby to start with? Could I be introducing too many signs at once?

Pick a few signs to start with. Make sure they are signs that you can use often with your baby. (Ex. Your child has MILK several times a day, or BATH is a sign that you can use consistently.) Use these first signs at **every** opportunity. However, feel free to sign BALL when your baby is playing with her ball or MUSIC when she gets excited to hear her favorite song! Don't worry about overloading your baby with too many signs. She hears words spoken all day. That's how babies learn!

How do I know if my baby is really producing a sign and not just playing with his hands?

There are several things to watch for and ask yourself when analyzing your baby's signs. Does your baby want something right now? Is he trying to tell you something? Recognizing your child's signs comes with time. When you see your baby doing what you think is a sign, pay attention to what they could be asking for or commenting on. If you think he may be signing MILK, watch for this movement the next few times your child is having MILK.

Many signs require the use of two hands. I'm a mom; my hands are always full! Should I wait until my hands are empty to show my baby the signs?

Many signs can be modified so that you can still sign when you have something in your hands. It is important to make sure that you are showing your baby the signs properly "when you can." However, don't let a great opportunity to model the MORE sign pass just because you have a baby in one hand. Do your best, and sign it with one hand!

My baby is signing "MORE" for everything! Does she not really know what it means, or what she is doing?

Most babies use their first sign for everything! They know that it is a way to communicate with you, so they use it whenever they want to draw your attention to something. For example, if your baby is signing MORE and you know that she really means MILK, respond enthusiastically anyway! "Good job honey! You want some MILK? Mommy will get you some MILK!" all the while signing MILK correctly to her!

All of my baby's signs look similar. How can I tell what he is trying to tell me or ask me?

When babies first start signing, many of their signs may look the same. They tend to stick with one hand shape or one location to do all of their signs. This is the same as when your baby starts speaking; many of his words may sound similar. It is important to pay attention to the context in which your baby is signing. Is your son asking for MORE, or is he telling you that he needs his DIAPER CHANGED?

My baby never pays attention to my signing! She seems way too busy! How can I teach her the signs if she won't even look at me?

Your baby may be paying attention even when you think that she is not! Do not stop signing to your baby just because you think she is not paying attention. Just as babies hear conversations that you think they don't hear, they are watching what you are doing much more often than you think!

Take advantage of the times when your baby's attention **is** on you. When she is in the highchair is often a great time.

She is going to be in one spot for a certain amount of time and you have something that she wants! Another great time is when she is in the bath. Again, she is in one spot and not going anywhere for a certain amount of time. Your daughter is in the bath and in close contact with you. Take advantage of these close-up, one-on-one opportunities!

Also, make sure that you are teaching your baby motivating signs. You want to always make sure that you are showing your baby signs for things that she will want to ask or tell you about.

3. Five Reasons to a Take Group Sign Language Class

Wondering if you want to take a class? Here are some reasons that might help you make up your mind:

Everyone learns best with a coach or mentor!

Think back to when you learned to drive a car. You had been a passenger in a car, and you probably read the driver's manual, but it was very helpful to have an experienced driver there to offer you support and suggestions when you first slid behind the wheel!

Learning the basics of signing with a baby is pretty easy. However, learning to sign with a professional baby sign language educator dedicated to teaching the best strategies for signing with your baby will make the learning process easier. It will be so much less stressful as you get the help you need to get it right the first time! By attending classes you will have so many helpful experiences; don't pass up the opportunity for one-on-one coaching and mentoring.

Get instant feedback on your own signing!

Signing is a motor skill that you learn just like swimming or riding a horse. If you practice the sign incorrectly, you will have a difficult time breaking your bad habits. Let a professional help you get it right from the very beginning!

Share the experience with like-minded people!

Everyone that you meet in your class will have a common goal: to learn how to effectively communicate with their babies before they can speak, using American Sign Language. Many on-going support groups and even sign supportive babysitting co-ops have been formed by participants in workshops and classes.

Enhance your sign language vocabulary!

With access to a baby sign language expert, you will be able to learn the signs that you might not find in the *SIGN with your BABY*™ book. Everyone needs to know the signs for special holidays and celebrations, or what if your baby's favorite fruit is papaya? You will be in luck; you will have access to a human sign language dictionary!

Experience the fun of learning activities designed specifically for you!

Parents, educators, or caregivers who are currently signing with babies and young children will be exposed to music, games, and toys that are designed to stimulate the learning process for babies and the adults who are signing with them. These activities will provide you with interactive and creative ways to incorporate signing into your daily life!

Section Two
SignShine®'s Families
Real Signing Stories

Signing Saved
Nathaniel from Cancer

W E STARTED SIGNING WITH NATHANIEL when he was six-months-old. We worked to make signing familiar words to him part of our routine, and he quickly picked up a few basic signs like "milk," "fan," and "bird." As Nathaniel got older, we continued signing with him and finger spelled words he saw frequently. He was fascinated by EXIT signs as a baby, and at just over a year old, he started signing his own approximation of "E X I T." Nathaniel continued to expand his signing and was able to recognize and sign all his colors and letters as well as dozens of other signs before he began to talk.

When Nathaniel was fifteen-months-old, he was diagnosed with neuroblastoma and had to spend quite a bit of time in the hospital for his treatment. During that time, signing was an incredible tool for him to communicate his needs and talk to us about what he saw around him. Being able to sign reduced his frustration tremendously because he could tell us what he needed before he could speak.

As Nathaniel has grown older and transitioned to verbal language he still enjoys signing. He is now helping us teach his baby sister signs so she'll have an early communication tool like he did.

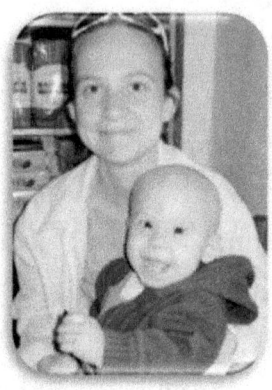

Bilingual Mother-In-Law

I ENROLLED MY SON JORDAN IN SignShine class when he was seven months old. I was looking for activities in which we could bond as a family by learning a new activity, and being a first time mom I wanted better way to communicate with my baby. My mother-in-law also attended the class. My mother-in-law primarily speaks Spanish. She cares for Jordan during the day. When Jordan signed "milk", "bath", or "more," my mother-in-law understood as well! Signing helped both of us relieve the frustration of trying to figure out what Jordan was communicating whether it was in Spanish or English. My mother-in-law found this extremely helpful and not frustrating as some grandparents might expect. The class exceeded my expectations; I learned how to communicate with my baby, and together we learned another language!

–Irlanda Mendez
Mom to a 3.5-year-old and a 2-year-old

Grandparents Appreciate Manners

I WANT TO SHARE A STORY about Violet when she was only 14-months-old. Violet and I were going to be joining my grandmother for a week long cruise. At the time, Violet could speak approximately 20 words and sign 20 words. There was some overlapping, and she had a total vocabulary of 30 words. My 80-year-old grandmother had expressed some reservation regarding some of my parenting, including the purpose of teaching Violet to sign. My grandmother's concerns were the same that I heard many other non-signers express.

At the first sit down dinner, which lasted 3 hours, Violet repeatedly signed "please" and "thank you." Those two magic words were not spoken until she was older. However, my grandmother was so impressed that a 14-month-old had manners and could express them. Over the week, my grandmother not only continued to encourage Violet to use all of her signs but was incredibly proud of her politeness, and my 80-year-old grandmother learned some signs as well.

– Laurie Bilgihan
Mom to 3 signing kids

A Sign of Hope

PEERING INTO MY JOURNAL WHICH not only has recorded memories on the pages I turn, but at the back of the book also has two pieces of loose papers that bring back memories. From a torn-out page of the journal once torn in two, there is a television drawn on one piece and an iPod with musical notes drawn on the other.

My nearly five year old son at the time was in the Intensive Care Unit at the hospital with a virus, which had caused his brain to swell. With the inflammation of his brain, it simultaneously affected his nervous system. After being sick at home, with what I thought was merely a cold, for three days, he was in the ICU not able to control his every day functioning skills such as lifting his arm, moving his hand, smiling, or being able to talk or walk. In the days that followed, as he was slowly regaining control of his motor skills, specifically that precious smile, I had drawn these two pictures. When I told him I was going to hold up each picture (the television to watch a DVD, or the iPod to listen to music and go to sleep), he immediately smiled as I held up the picture of the television.

Then he began regaining control of his hands but still was not able to speak freely. And just as I used the pictures and his smile to communicate before, he was able to use sign language to express his wants and needs. The language that allowed for us to communicate before he could speak as a toddler was the same language that brought us together when he was striving to regain his full ability to communicate at the age of four.

Signing was the language that continued to bond us together through simple means in what could had been a very frustrating experience were it not for the power of communicating through signing.

The pages of my journal continue to turn within my reach, and I recall these precious memories of communicating through the power of signing. I had three "Thomas the

Trains" DVDs to choose from. I began to hold up the three and figure out how to have him choose which one. As I was saying the colors of the DVD cases, I saw him hold up his hand and move his thumb in and then slowly begin to move his hand. He was signing "blue." I remembered all the pictures the speech pathologist had printed out such as those of a boy "sleeping," "watching TV," "playing cars," and so forth. I thought how much easier it would be for him to sign instead of trying to point to the little pictures. As I was going over each picture and trying to see if he could sign them, I saw his hand go up and try to sign "TV." He was basically telling me, "Be quiet, Mom. I just want to relax and watch TV already."At that time, when he was done watching, he looked over at me. I got up and went over to his bed to ask as I signed, "Do you want a new one or same one?" I began to sign more words as I spoke. He took his other hand from underneath the blanket and attempted to sign "new" as his hands came together on top of each other. Then I asked which kind of DVD. He was able to sign "trains" to tell me that he wanted to watch another "Thomas the Train" DVD following with the sign "red" for the red case. It was clear as he signed. He smiled as I grabbed the red DVD and placed it in the player. I could not help but jump inside as I realized what a blessing signing was at that moment in time in our lives. It was allowing me to clearly see my son's needs at a time in his life when he was striving to be so brave and strong! And as I asked if he was feeling alright in the words "Are you good?" I remember him signing "good." It was a time in our lives where signing helped create signs of hope. I have since continued to record memories as my son made a full recovery and is a healthy young seven year old boy in the first grade, still enjoying a "Thomas the Train" DVD from time to time!

–Shawn Tran and Truwin

Alex Signs
Concept of More

ALEX WAS SIGNING FOR "MORE" food when he was around 10 months. Then, he used that sign any time he wanted anything such as: "more" milk, "more" food, "more" car, etc. He didn't really seem to pick up any other signs for a couple months, but I remembered reading about a similar experience from another SignShine mother so I wasn't too concerned. Then, right around his first birthday, something must have just clicked, and he started attempting to sign more. He signed "all done" when he wasn't hungry anymore or when a toy was done playing a song. He started signing "eat" (by pointing to his mouth) whenever he wanted food or a snack. He signed "milk" (by wiggling his fingers slowly into a fist). He began signing parts of songs with me. (Singing/signing was part of our bedtime/naptime ritual. I sang/signed while he drank from his bottle. I wasn't sure, but now I know that he really was paying attention and watching!) He would sign "star," point to the "sky," and wonder "what" you are. He would also sign the beginning part to itsy bitsy spider any time he heard the song, whether it was me singing or one of his toys playing the tune.

Another thing that amazed me was that I was reading a book to him one day, and he started doing the twinkle of the "star" sign and I didn't know why at first. Then I realized that the story I was reading had the word "twinkle" in it and he had heard the word and signed "star." I've also noticed that he's using his own "sign language" to try to communicate with me more, whether it is pointing to where he wants to go, or hitting his head on the table to recreate how he got his ouchy when I ask him what happened. I feel much closer to him because he knows that I understand what he is trying to tell me, and he gets so excited when he realizes that we've communicated. I can't wait for tomorrow to see what he will do next! (I am hoping that another sign that he learns soon is "pain" because I would feel much better if he could tell me if he hurts.)

...Alex Continues to Sign

*E*MAIL KAREN SENT ME A *few months later:*
I just wanted to share the story of Alex's first sign. He just turned 10 months, and he's been imitating things that I do and sounds that I make lately. (Clapping, kissing, coughing, yelling, short words, laughing, and yes, even burping.) I've been asking him if he wants more when I've been feeding him and doing the "more" sign. He started copying me on Tuesday, and I made sure to quickly give him more of his food. He finally got it that whenever he did the sign he would quickly get more food. I wasn't sure at first that that was what he was doing because he doesn't use his fingertips...it looks more like a clap but he does it very purposefully and just does it 2 or 3 times. (It kinda reminds me of somebody trying to use "The Clapper".....ha ha!) He may think that it means he "wants" something because he did it today when I asked him if he wanted his milk. I am very ex-

cited that he wants to communicate with me, and he seems very excited too that I understand him! I'm so looking forward to his next signs....Thanks again for a great class!

–Karen and Alexander

Daddy and Me

Brooklyn, 9m, signs DADDY

MY HUSBAND AND I STARTED taking our daughter to SignShine classes when she was six months old. We are so glad that we chose this class over any other parent and me class. Brooklyn started signing "milk" within a week of starting the class, and shortly after, more signs followed. By the time she was one year old, she was signing 17 different words or phrases, and she was very verbal. I really believe that SignShine was what helped with her being so verbal. Speaking to her and signing at the same time made her language skills blossom. We were also able to use sign language as a bridge for teaching her Spanish.

Going for walks or reading books with her is so much fun because we get to see her express herself and we are able to communicate with her, often she reads the books to us! Every day before her daddy goes to work, she signs "I love you" and "I miss you." Without SignShine, she would have never learned how to say that.

Thank You, Etel, and your wonderful teachers for being so nurturing and teaching sign language in such a wonderful way!

–Lucy, Santiago Gonzalez

Aiden Uses his Signs

THE DOCTOR: Aiden was maybe 13 months old. I had been signing with him from birth. The ABC's signed and sung would calm him down every time and "Twinkle Twinkle" became a car favorite for a high energy kiddo in a car seat. Well, one day he seemed to have a kind of uncomfortable look on his face every time he had to go pee pee. As I was changing his diaper, he signed HURT above his penis. I then asked him "Does it HURT when you go PEE PEE?" and he signed "YES" So, off to the doctor thinking this little one is getting a UTI. We get to the doctor's office, and once he got up on the table and his vitals were taken, the doctor asked me why I thought that Aiden was beginning to get a UTI. I said, "He told me." The doctor looked at me a little sideways and asked me "What do you mean?" I said," Ask him." So, the doctor, with a puzzled look on his face, asked this little 13-month-old, "Where does it hurt?" Aiden then signed HURT above his penis. The doctor looked at me and asked if that was the sign for "hurt" and I said, "yes."

After taking a urine sample, we found that he had the beginnings of a UTI, and we were able to treat it homeopathically, avoiding antibiotics simply because Aiden had the tools to tell me and the doctor what was going on with his body. The doctor said as we were leaving that he wished all non-speaking kiddos could sign and how much easier it would make his job.

The Teacher: Aiden is now almost 4 years old and has started at a new preschool in a new state. We had moved from California to Utah. He is a very confident, funny, creative, and a tad bossy child. We had been doing a countdown to starting school. At his old school in CA, I was able to go in weekly and read and sign a story to the kids in his class. The teachers loved it and found that for the little ones who were shy or not talking that much (It was a group of 2-year-olds.) would sign PLEASE or THANK YOU or an animal or color to indicate a book they wanted to read or a crayon they wanted.

But I digress, because upon knowing he was going to start this new school, Aiden's first question was if the teachers were going to be able to sign? I told him "No, but maybe I can talk to them and see if I can come in and read like I used to do at the other school." He looked at me like he was thinking up a storm and off he went to go color. The first day of school came, and off I went with a very excited boy. We got to school and walked in. I introduced him to his teacher, and he introduced himself with his name sign and no words. She looked at me, and I explained that he signed and that was his name sign. She said "Hi Aiden, are you excited???" He looked up at me and then back to her and said, "I am going to teach you sign. This is A, B, C, D, GREEN. I love green; it's my favorite color. I also like DINOSAURS. This is the sign DINOSAUR." and then did his biggest Dino roar he could do. The teacher was looking at me and laughing and said, "I guess I am going to be learning some signs!"

DINOSAURS: Aiden loves dinosaurs. At 3.5 yrs old, he says he wants to grow up to be a paleontologist and can name about 30 different dinosaurs. He started to read around 3 and loves spelling words. We are in a major finger spelling place in our lives right now. His new "favorite" Dino is the Micropachycephalosaurus. Yes, he can say it, and I can not. This is the longest dino name out of all the dinos. He insists on having me finger spell it about a dozen times every night while reading his favorite dino book. I think he just loves to see me struggle with trying to spell it and all those letters.

ME: I love signing. I love anything that can give a child a sense of empowerment. It probably goes back to when I was a child in 4th grade and felt my first sense of disempowerment and then finding it again. I grew up in Utah in a very LDS neighborhood, and I was not LDS. I had attended a private Episcopalian school up until 3rd grade. I then had decided I really wanted to get to know the kids in the neighborhood and the best way for me to do this was to go to the public school down the street where all the kids in the neighborhood went.

My parents were not exactly for this idea, but I was insistent. I wanted friends so badly to play with in the neighborhood. So, for fourth grade, I got to go. I was sooo excited. It didn't take long to find out I was the odd man out, being all the kids were LDS and I was not. I didn't see what the big deal was, but apparently to some of the girls (the ones I really wanted to play with) this difference made me a target. I was being called names that you would normally only hear adults say. I was teased and singled out simply because I was not LDS. I became very sad and lonely.

One day while playing alone on the monkey bars, the special needs class was let out for recess. A few of the deaf kids started playing on the bars next to me. They were not saying anything to me, and I assumed that they were just going to be like the others. Then I saw them signing to each other and trying to vocalize. This situation made me feel better knowing that they were not talking to me because I would have a hard time understanding them. We continued playing next to each other and then I heard one of them get very agitated. They were all looking all over the ground for something. I came over to see if I could help. They were looking for a hearing aid that had fallen off one of the kids while they were doing flips on the bars. When a hearing aid falls off, it creates a high-pitched sound so it can be found. They were having a hard time locating it, and I was able to find it. After I handed it back to the owner, they grabbed my hand and dragged me into their classroom to tell their teacher. She explained to me that they had wanted to say thank you and how much they appreciated me helping them, being most hearing kids wouldn't. Kids can be mean.

From that point on, I had some friends. They and their teacher taught me some signs, and I learned the alphabet from my brother's Boy Scout hand book so we could talk. I left school that day feeling so good that not only I could help someone but that these kids only cared that I was a kind person that accepted them just as they were and they accepted me, just as I was. Those kids empowered me. They gave me one of the greatest lessons in my life and fueled a passion for Sign Language.

Later in life I went to college to study Deaf Studies and to really learn ASL. This lead to my understanding of the power it can give an infant or child with learning disabilities such as Autism or Down syndrome and ultimately lead to my teaching Sign Language for babies and their parents. Though I had returned to private school the following year, I never forgot or will forget those children and the sense of self these children had. In teaching my son ASL from birth I have had the honor and the occasional frustration of watching my infant develop into a self aware, creative, and curious, 3.5 yr old boy with a passion for learning and a sense of no limitations as to what he can do.

He has taught me how to move through fear and how to live in the moment with passion and openness to learn whatever the moment has to teach. He is bossy and stubborn and when he gets angry he communicates these feelings freely, and when he can't find the words he has the signs. What a gift for both of us!

–Danielle Hogle and Aidan

My Special Benefits of Signing

SIGNING WITH MY BABY WAS the single best thing I ever did for her. We started when my daughter (Luci) was 6 months and have been doing ever since. Luci is now 4 years old and still signing. Of course, there are the regular benefits of signing like Luci has always been able to ask for the food she wants. But the special part of signing with Luci is that I got to see the world from her point of view long before she spoke words. She would point out things she saw in a store or even in the sky. Luci has always loved animals, and one of her favorite activities has always been walking through pet stores and signing the animals. I have been blessed enough to see the world from her eyes since she was 9 months. How many people can say that?

Another reward that I have received is the gift of knowing how Luci feels. As soon as I learned the signs for emotions, I started using them like crazy with Luci. I think that this has always given her the freedom to be open with her feelings. She continues sign to me her feelings and is very open at sharing her feelings with those around her. A couple of years ago we had some major changes to our family, and through it all Luci has been able to tell me how she feels. She recognizes her emotions, acknowledges them and shares them. Most adults can't do that, but my Luci could at 2 years. Today Luci and I still sign together. It comes in very handy in our everyday lives, crowded places, over long distances, when I need to tell her something that everyone around us doesn't need to hear, and best of all when we are places where we can't talk to each other.

–Natali Guadarrama-Plotner and Luci

Introducing Signs

During my pregnancy, I read several books about the benefits of teaching sign language to hearing babies and found it fascinating. As soon as my twins were born, I started introducing sign language to them – basic signs that I learned from books. Of course, I had no idea if I was doing the signs properly or what signs I should introduce next. So when they reached 10 months old, I decided to seek professional guidance and enrolled in a SignShine class. Since that time, we've taken several sessions which have been completely amazing. Not only do they have fabulous teachers that engage the children, but it's also great fun to socialize with the other families. And the children absolutely love it...the songs, the games, and all the special attention!

SignShine has given us so much in helping us get started with our children's education and providing them with a strong foundation – fabulous classes as well as ongoing interaction with the teachers via email and downloadable tools that have helped us in working with our twins at home. And, while as adults we understand the benefits of education, to them it's just play time and fun activities to keep their active and developing minds entertained. What a gift to have ASL be a part of their daily lives and keep them from being bored. As a result, we have much happier children.

My twins are now 16 months old and have a sign vocabulary of over 60 words including some phrases and an understanding of putting signs together to create a thought. With the help of SignShine, we've given our children the gift of communicating with us and each other using ASL. I'm beyond amazed at what they have expressed through signing – from what they want to eat, to what activities they like, what they see, and how they feel. And above all, the best part is looking at their faces when they realize that they've been able to communicate with you! The smiles let you know, "Thank you for understanding me. What a relief!"

–Pamela Yager
Mommy to twins

Daddy's Reaction to Signing... The Miracle

WHEN I WAS PREGNANT WITH my daughter, my son and I were taking SignShine together. We started when he was about 6 months old. My husband was very skeptical but thought it was a harmless way for us to pass the time together in a group setting. One night, when my son probably about a year old, we were talking about the new baby that was coming, and I pointed to my belly. My son signed "baby"! My husband was amazed. It was a thrilling moment for us all and proof that we were doing more than just passing time at SignShine.

I cannot begin to count the times we use sign language in our house. We all sign "I love you"...just this morning, my 22-month-old daughter (the "baby" in my belly in the above example) signed "I love you" to my 9-year-old on his way to school. Talk about a tender moment! We regularly use sign language to make choices on what to eat; my 22-month-old daughter's favorite signs are, of course, "more" and "food/

eat"! My now 3-year-old son knows everything from "stop," to numerous animals, aircrafts (airplane, helicopter), both of my toddlers regularly (thank you, Etel!) use the signs "please" and "thank you." When we read, we try to sign as much as we know along with the stories, and of course, my children love signing along while we are singing songs.

I believe having this skill has given us a richer bond, and encouraged vocabulary development in my children, especially my 3-year-old*. Even if they are not able to speak a word, if I sign a complete sentence to them, they can respond with a "yes" or "no". We role play using sign language and dolls about feelings, and it really seems to help them work through tough moments without having situations escalate.

I am so grateful to know Etel and for her sharing the magic of sign language with me and our family. I recommend signing with your child to everyone. It is simply another way to connect and communicate with your loved ones.

*My 9-year-old is extraordinarily bright, scoring in the 99th% on standardized tests since he started taking them a few years ago, and I do not recall his vocabulary being as extensive at this age. I am not a scientist and cannot make scientific claims, but I have to say my 3-year-old's vocabulary is amazing (to me), and I do not think signing hampered his development in any way ~ quite the contrary.

−Tracci Shibuya and David

Signing Eases Terrible Twos for a Single Mom

MY DAUGHTER AVERY STARTED TO take classes of signing when she was six months of age. It was wonderful to see my daughter sign because it allow me to understand what were her needs since she was not able to speak at the time. It was amazing seeing her first sign MILK. It was from this moment that enabled me to comfort her easily by giving her the items that she was directly asking for, rather than having to hear her cry for something. Having Avery sign at the age of two helped her to pass the "terrible twos." Rather than facing the difficulty of "terrible twos," signing made her age easy by presenting more opportunity to just have FUN.

For Avery, sign language not only became her second language, but it was also a pathway for her motor skill development. Avery's sign language facilitated 3rd language learning. Now I am proud to say that my daughter Avery has a third language: Spanish.

For Avery, signing became part of her life. Now that she is, four some of the words have still stayed with her even though there was not a constant reinforcement. She now recognizes the words she sees, and she feels excited to know that she knows it all by herself.

One of the best benefits that signing created for me and my daughter is that we share time together as one. Signing provided a time to get to know each other, such as what we like and what we dislike. It also was her first baby class. It was a moment that I will never forget, and now that I am writing about this, it brings tears to my eyes because it was a moment when she was my little baby. It was a time when she met other kids and had fun with them by practicing her signing words.

–Avery's Mom

Sebastian's Head Start

My son Sebastian started group "signing" classes at a local store when he was 14 months old. I was intrigued with the idea of giving my son a way to communicate before he had the ability to speak, but I was unprepared for how much fun the classes were. They became (and still are) the highlight of his week! We now study privately, and he is 23 months old. Very soon after he started, he began "signing" the word "more," letting us know when he wanted more formula, another hug, or a continuation of whatever silly game his father and I were in the midst of to make him laugh. His first spoken words were still many months away, but I will always think of those "mores" as our first "conversations."

−Tina
Sebastian's Mom

Eugene's Miracle

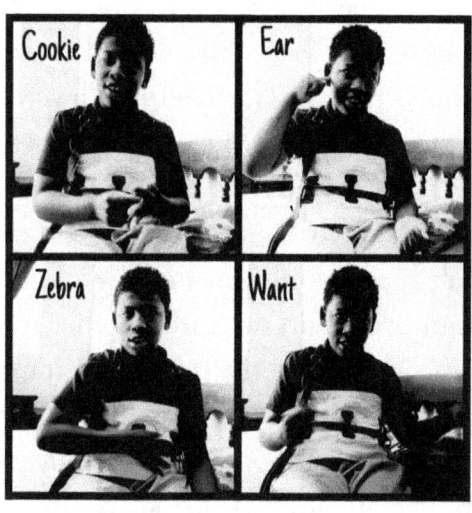

I CAME TO SIGNSHINE IN SEARCH of options for my son Eugene who is diagnosed as developmentally delayed. While Eugene has made great strides in the area of walking, he still struggles in the area of speech communication. Prior to coming to SignShine Eugene received little if any instruction in signing from LAUSD. Rather they focused on PECS although he never uses his communication device to my knowledge in the classroom. Unfortunately, his teacher does not sign. As a parent, I have been opposed to PECS because I felt that he needs a valid language to utilize and allow his neurons to develop.

I believe Eugene has comprehension of approximately fifty words. He uses approximations of signs rather than the actual sign. This is, I believe, due to his disability, cerebral palsy. Interestingly in Eugene's case since attending SignShine classes, his speech communication has begun to be discernable. Each day I hear with more clarity actual words coming from him. He has said recently "I love you!" "You're mean!" and yesterday, he said "Daddy!" clearly.

In today's economy, lessons are really a struggle to pay for; however, the benefit far outweighs the struggle. I am so pleased each time he talks to me. While I want to see Eugene communicate, I do not care whether it is through a combination of signs and verbalization. I simply want him to communicate and help to lesson his frustration level. He has benefited in so many areas. His ability to focus and concentrate has greatly increased since coming, and his enthusiasm for learning is really fun to watch as he greets his instructor when she walks through our front door. Eugene communicates through strategies that the world should attempt to understand in order to allow children with disabilities access to experiences that benefit the development of the whole child. We owe this ability to SignShine.

–Sheila Love
Mom to Eugene, 6 years old

Our SignShine Story

My baby Maxwell and I started SignShine classes when he was ten weeks old. I remember calling Etel nervously to ask if that was too early. So many 'baby' classes want you to wait until your baby is six months old. But in our case, it was very important for me that we start as early as possible.

Due to severe complications during Max's delivery, he suffered significant brain damage. So significant that the entire left side of his brain is basically non-functioning. Additionally, a stroke centered in the speech/language center of the brain puts him at great risk of having a speech delay. After spending four weeks in the NICU, I brought my baby home willing to do anything to help get him back on the right track. I was so thrilled when Etel said I could start signing classes with my baby at such a young age. If his speech was going to be delayed, I knew offering him the option of signing would at the very least allow him a means of communication.

At this time, Max and I have taken 12 weeks of Baby Signing classes together. I can't believe how much I have learned. I sign as much as possible to Max. He is just over seven months old, and a few days ago I am certain I saw him sign-babbling. Although I couldn't quite make out what he was trying to sign, much like when a baby begins to talk-babble, I knew he was trying to communicate.

So far, Max is proving to be quite the miracle. He is developmentally on track and even is making verbal sounds appropriate for his age-level. But we're still not sure about his speech. I feel so grateful to SignShine knowing that regardless of whether there are delays or not, Max will be able to "tell" me what he needs, wants, thinks, or feels.

—Erin Musick

Understanding Language Before Verbal Words

LEARNING AND PRACTICING SIGN LANGUAGE with our daughter Violette Skye has been an amazing journey for our family. It opened a doorway of communication that may have been lost and allowed us all to connect in a joyous and fun way. We feel that signing has helped our baby from getting frustrated. For example, she has been able to sign to us that she needed her diaper changed, that she wanted to read books, or dance, or wanted water or food. How beautiful of an experience for us all!

Our parents, family, and friends have been in awe of Violettes' understanding and have had a great time learning sign language themselves. I think it is a testimony to how brilliant babies and children are and how we possibly underestimate their wisdom.

We also wonder how learning has affected her brain development. It is learning a second language and is visual as well as physical. This can only have a positive affect on a child's development.

We thank you for your continued work in developing sign language programs and education and wish you blessings.
Thank you,

-Lisa Marie, Jessie and
Viollette Goodwein-Rice

Section Three
Pictorial Dictionary

Cheat Sheet
© Copyright 2015 SignShine

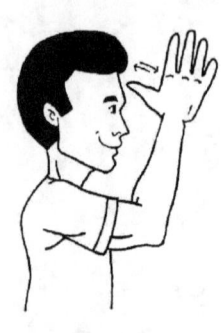
DAD

MOM

BABY

MILK

EAT

READY

MUSIC

BATH

I LOVE YOU

LOVE FRIEND SHARE

PLAY BALL BOOK

SIGN DIAPER SLEEP

Family Signs

Boy

Girl

Dad

Mom

Eat

Drink

Apple

Cheese

Milk

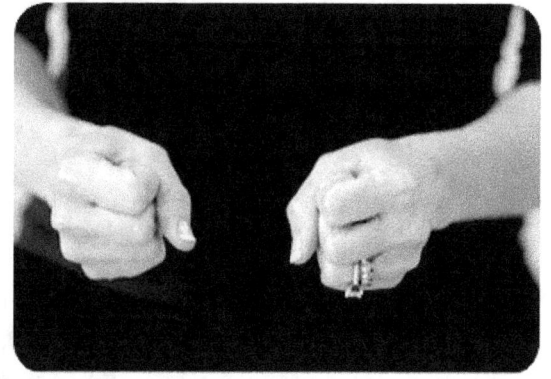

Candy

1

2

Cookie

1

2
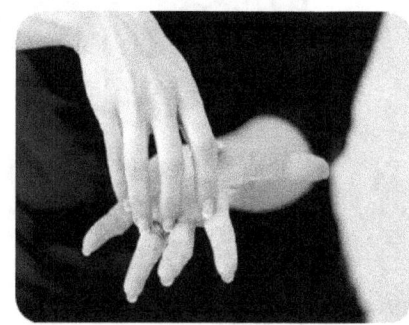

Cake

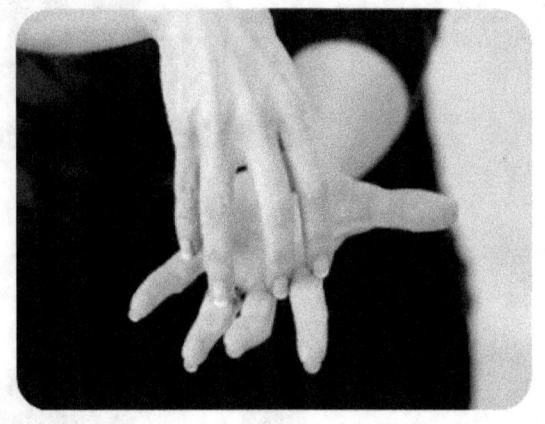

162   Etel Leit

Concept Signs

More

1

2
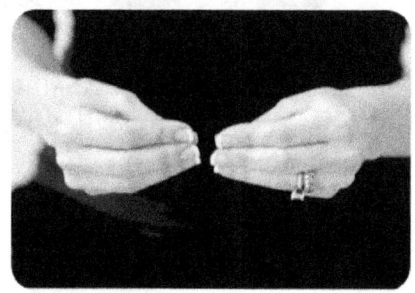

Thank You

(Move your hand toward the person)

Playtime Signs

Slide

1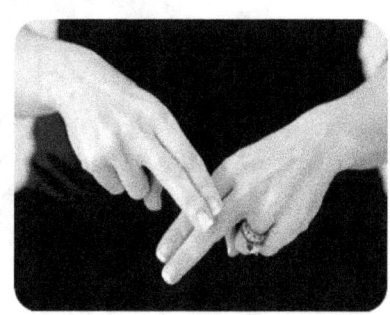

2

Ball

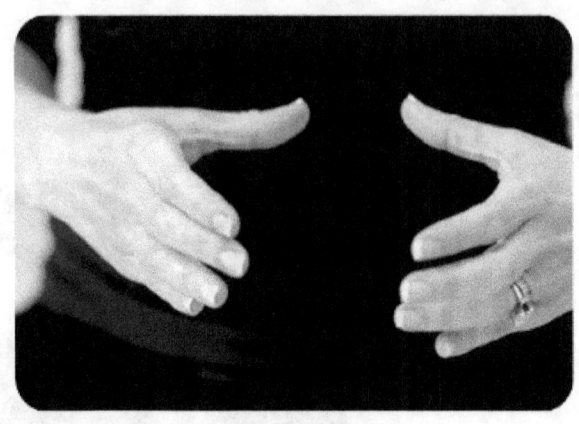

Jump

Telephone

Turtle (Hide)

Hippo

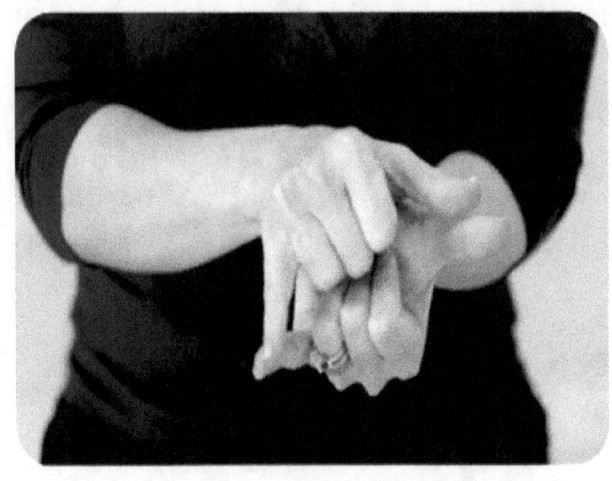

Stand

Socks

1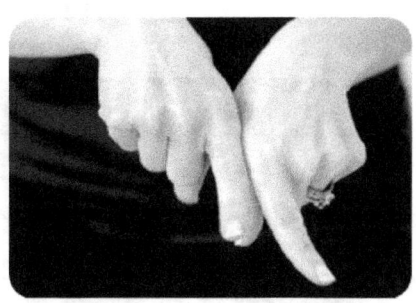

2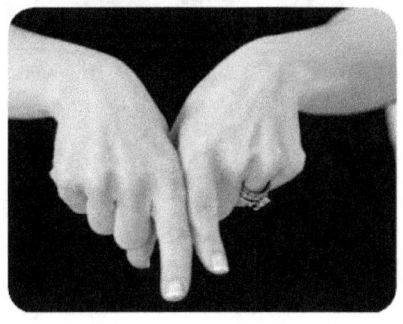

Shoes

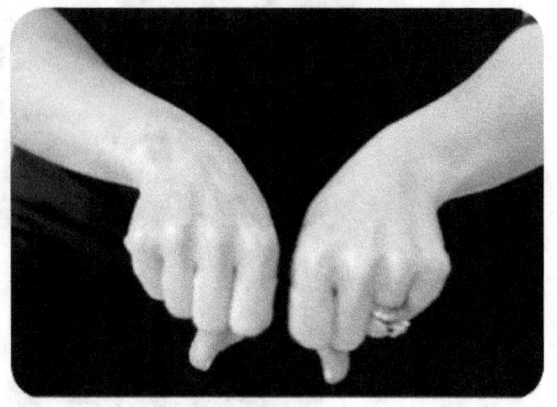

Etel Leit

Bedtime Signs

Bed

Book

Awake

1

2

Music or Sing

Sign

Time

Color Signs

Black

Brown

Blue

Green

Red

1

2

Pink

Feeling & Emotion Signs

Bored

Frustrated

Worried

Scared

Surprised

Happy

Excited

Silly

I Love You

Section Four
Your Signing Story

My Signing Story

Child's Name:

Child's Photo

Date of Birth:

Inspired to Sign by: _____

First Sign We Sign: _____
Age: _____

First Sign Was Recognized: _____
Age _____

First Sign Signed: _____
Age: _____

Favorite Sign:

My Signing Story

My Signing Story

Functional Signs:

Fun Signs:

Feeling Signs:

www.ingramcontent.com/pod-product-compliance
Lightning Source LLC
Chambersburg PA
CBHW050637300426
44112CB00012B/1828